EDUCATION THAT WORKS

The Neuroscience of Building a
More Effective Higher Education

Dr. James Stellar
Senior University Leader | Neuroscientist | Cocaine Researcher

IDEAPRESS
PUBLISHING

A Note to the Reader

I happily followed my father's footsteps to become a professor of neuroscience and, ultimately, a chief academic officer, at a major public research university. It was the family business. Even so, when I talk with friends, particularly those outside the university space, many of them think that higher education is smart, but also a total ivory-tower system, disconnected from the real world. So do some of our students' employers and many of our critics. Maybe you do too. That is why I began this note by stating what I see as the problem.

Ironically, the solution to this perceived ivory-tower problem is as old as the history of the university and as modern as its current practice. It comes, simply enough, from complementing classical course-based education with direct, high-impact experiences outside the classroom, in internships, service-learning, study abroad, undergraduate research, entrepreneurship, real-world capstone projects, and so on. We call that practice experiential education, and Chapters 7 through 13 in this book discuss how it works or could work in higher education today. The last two chapters, Chapters 14 and 15, try to apply those ideas to the university or college structure.

There is something else that I think makes this book interesting, and I want to discuss it first. As a professor of neuroscience, I believe there is a natural reason for the maturing effect of experiential education on our students. It comes from how the brain is built. You see, despite the feeling that our conscious self is in charge of everything we do, much of what we decide to do occurs outside of our awareness in ancient brain circuits. This is what we call unconscious decision-making. It is an old concept that is alive now as modern brain scanners studies show activity patterns in economic and other types of decisions, perhaps even someday in the choice of a college major.

I think you need to know how this unconscious decision making works, so the first major section of this book (Chapters 3 through 6) is on that topic. If you already know some neuroscience, perhaps from a college course, you might want to begin with Chapters 5 and 6. But I do not recommend skipping those chapters, as they provide the basis for the perspective taken thereafter.

I wrote this book for anyone interested in the higher education system, but particularly those in the United States, where my perspective is the richest. (I have traveled enough to know that there are other perspectives, but I do not address them specifically here.) I have tried to make everything in the book, even the neuroscience, accessible to the lay audience, and I hope I succeeded.

This book grew out of a blog that began 2009. I wrote it with some colleagues, but largely with students, whose insights are often fascinating and typically revealing. I tried to include their voices by citing some of these blog posts in the footnotes. I find the student voice to be overwhelmingly optimistic, even if it is full of ideas for improvements. For students, I felt compelled to write this book to add something critical but positive to the debate on direction of higher education today.

Finally, please read this book as one part higher education, one part neuroscience, and one part personal reflection over a long career. Note that there are many scholars who have devoted their academic careers to research in higher education while I was in the laboratory doing basic neuroscience research. I am influenced by them, but held back on citations to them to keep this book focused on a general audience. I encourage you to follow my notes or even just search online if a topic I mention or a book I cite interests you.

We in higher education need to address both processes of the mind: the conscious, rational, verbal; and the unconscious, emotional, instinctive—to get the maximum impact for our students. Referring to these two processes, I like to say that we have to "row the boat with both oars." It is simply brain smart to do so.

Dedication

To my wife, Teresa, to our daughters, Jenny and Devrie, and to the whole family who allowed me some of their time to develop and write this book.

Contents

Preface

It is clear to even the casual observer that American higher education needs to change. Despite its great strengths and historic contributions, the industry is criticized for charging too much and delivering too little. New books on this topic abound, from *Academically Adrift: Limited Learning on College Campuses* (Arum and Roska, 2011), to *Higher Education: How Colleges Are Wasting Our Money and Failing Our Kids—and What We Can Do About It* (Hacker and Dreifus, 2010) to Kevin Cary's 2015 book, *The End of College: Creating the Future of Learning and the University of Everywhere*. These newer works take their place next to older counterparts, like *Prof Scam: Professors and the Demise of Higher Education* by Charles Sykes (1988).

All of them, and many more I did not cite, argue that colleges' priorities have become distorted and do not serve the modern world well. That opinion is echoed by a steady chorus of criticism from industry, government, and a broader accountability movement, particularly in America. Industry often says that college graduates cannot write well, think critically, or work effectively in teams.

On the price side, student debt is now at record levels. Higher-education tuition has increased almost ten-fold in the since I became an assistant professor of neuroscience in 1978 at Harvard University in the Department of Psychology. By contrast, the annual average rate of inflation over much the same period has driven up prices about three-fold. Several years ago student loan debt in America exceeded one trillion dollars.

Yet I remain optimistic.

While I may have started my career as a professor, in 1998 I entered the ranks of senior academic administration by becoming dean of the College of Arts and Sciences at Northeastern University. In 2009, I moved to the public side of higher education by holding two provost positions, first at Queens College CUNY and now at the University at Albany SUNY, where I was appointed in the fall of 2016 as interim president. Along the way, I had professorial and administrative experiences that suggested an approach to help higher education today be more effective, even if it could not help it be less expensive.

That approach is to tie classical higher-education, classroom-based facts and theories to learning from direct experience in places outside the college in internships, study abroad, service-learning, undergraduate research, and so on. Some of us call this approach *experiential education* and no one is more surprised than me to see it resting on modern research into how the brain works. As we will see, that research may even explain why higher education largely missed this approach until now, continuing instead to rely on what some call an ivory-tower route to education.

To give the briefest discussion now of what will consume much of the book, I find it interesting that in 2002, Daniel Kahneman, a Princeton University psychologist, won the Nobel Prize in economics for showing that the economic models of market function, widely assumed to be rational, were missing a kind of decision-making behavior that was not so rational, despite being predictable and understandable. His 2011 book, *Thinking Fast and Slow*, makes the point that we think in two ways. The fast way is automatic, intuitive, and uses tacit knowledge more than the explicit facts and theories about which we can easily speak from our rational minds. I believe that this form of unconscious decision-making is what neuroscientist David Eagleman refers to in the title of his 2011 book, *Incognito: The Secret Lives of the Brain*. Finally, I believe we can apply the lessons from these two books to higher education in a very natural way and that application is experiential education.

I have seen experiential education work in two ways. First, as a professor at Northeastern University, I saw my undergraduate research assistants use a paid internship program called cooperative education, to do high-level research in my laboratory and succeed in getting into medical and graduate schools at a level that was comparable to my earlier undergraduates at Harvard University. At an institutional level, as dean of the College of Arts and Sciences at Northeastern University, I was part of a senior leadership team that leveraged experiential education to help the university achieve a remarkable rise in the *U.S. News & World Report* rankings, from about 165 to a peak of 39. More importantly, the university attracted one of the largest applicant pools of all private universities in America, with more than 45,000 applicants seeking some 2,800 seats. Through my work as a co-founder and co-director of a summer institute designed to develop experiential-education programs, I have seen this approach work at more than eighty other universities and colleges over the past ten years. I know this approach works and I want to show you why.

Acknowledgments

I developed many of the ideas in this book by writing a blog called "The Other Lobe of the Brain." It began in 2009, largely with students who shared personal experiences as well as their research thinking. The blog can be found at www.otherlobe.com. The first post is with my former undergraduate, Shwen Gwee, who also set up the original web page. Many posts followed, and the list of blog co-authors grew.[1]

1 The blog co-authors who are cited in this book are: Golshan Aghanori, Nawal Ali, Cynthia Bainton, Alicia Barrientos, Stephanie Bermudez, Lauren Blachorsky, Ashley Bryant, Agata Buras, Christina Calixte, Danielle Capalbo, Tiffany Caputo, Vanessa Castro, Carly Chierico, Marc Cohen, Natania Crane, Raquel De Leon, Lauren Donohoe, Adrienne Dooley, Naomi Ducat, Rachel Eager, Brittanyliz Echevarria, Avani Enot, Voula Galanopoulos, Alexandra Gulyan, Maria Graceffa, Alexandra Hilbert, Tehya Johnson, Shiela Kern, Jungyo Kim, Laura Klipp, Shoshana Korman, Paulina Kulesza, Bronwyn Lommel, Joanne Lund-Pops, Amanda Marsden, Chrisel Martinez, Antonella Mason, Lara Milane, Eric Miller, Emily Monoco, Ilyssa Monda, Carolina Morgan, Kristen Morin, Kristen Moussalli, Sanaa Mylan, Naveen Naqvi, Edna Normand, Catherine Nunez, Jessica Olson, Stephanie Ortiz, Swapna Rao Patel, Laura Pinzon, Ashley Pira, Sarah Platt, Lara Porter, Richard Porter, Darya Rubenstein, Allyson Savin, Andi Sciacca, Gregory Sholette, Sophie Shrand, Ajay Singh, Jessica Singh, Shalini Singh, Paulina Smietanka, Raphael Spiro, Ashley Stemple, Alissa Shugats-Cummings, Tricia Tiu, Arielle Torra, Michaela Tralli,

One paper I wrote with two colleagues from Northeastern University: one, a student at the time, Amanda Marsden; the other, a professor and former Vice President for Cooperative Education, Rick Porter.[2] We put it up as the second blog post. I thank them for really getting me started.

Since the inception of The Other Lobe, I have worked with Adrienne Dooley. She wrote the third blog post with me in 2009 and set the format for all the posts that followed, which focused heavily on undergraduate co-authors. After all, as she argued, we are talking about their education. When the blog turned into a book project, she helped organize an initial major research effort with students and colleagues and then helped me develop a private website chat room where many of the ideas in this book were discussed and developed. Perhaps most importantly, she was a consistent, optimistic force over the last six years.

Finally, I want to thank my publisher, IdeaPress, and its founder, Rohit Bhargava, for encouragement and for shaping the title and cover design, as well as the whole project. He hired an editor, Andrew Trotter, to polish my writing, and that made the book even better.

Marina Vazura, Chloé Skye Weiser, Ute Wenkemann, Anna Wilga, Erin Williams.
2 Blog Footnote 1.   http://otherlobe.com/learning-outside-the-traditional-classroom-educating-the-whole-student/

CHAPTER 1:

What Is Experiential Education? An Answer in Three Stories

Experiential education is a broad term for a broad range of, well, experiences that help students learn about a subject from the perspective of doing, not just receiving knowledge and giving it back in the classroom. Common experiential education programs at the college and university level include student internships, study abroad, undergraduate research, service-learning, fieldwork, entrepreneurship and even some volunteer activities. The work-based internship form is practiced all over the world and sometimes is called by other names, such as work-integrated learning (WIL) or cooperative and work-integrated education (CWIE). Herman Schneider, the founder of the first work-education program in United States, called it *cooperative education*. His program was established at the University of Cincinnati, over 100 years ago, to focus particularly on internships. In 1926, he became the first president of the Association of Cooperative Colleges and his term of *cooperative education* is still widely used particularly in the United States and Canada.[1]

We will return to definitions in the next chapter, but here I want to again make the point that I mentioned in the preface: All forms of experiential education tap into an often overlooked form of mental processing called unconscious decision-making, which occurs in an older part of our brain. Often we are aware of that processing only when we notice that a decision feels right, or alternatively, it feels like one has made a bad choice. We want this experience for our students, hopefully positive, while they are in college. We want to help them see the value of a chosen major, or to switch and find the one that is right for them. We want them to grow and develop into more mature learners who can fit into the workplace at graduation or seek even more education and know why they are doing it.

I also want to mention that experiential education often requires students to work in groups. The group approach delivers other important aspects of a quality higher education, such as developing teamwork skills that industry particularly prizes after graduation. Back on campus, when students develop true teamwork, and thereby shape and raise one another's expectations, they become more interested in their subject and show a greater commitment toward completing their studies through to graduation.

Can universities design programs that make that kind of growth possible for students in college? How should administrators design them? What factors make them work, including those factors in our brains and behavior? How do we get students out of the ivory tower to do that, and how can the faculty create some of the same kinds of powerful opportunities within the ivory tower? This book will try to answer those questions. But, let's start with a personal story.

---

1 http://www.cafce.ca, http://www.ceiainc.org/about/, http://www.waceinc.org

A Story of Personal Transformation

I went to meet Mariko at the student union at Northeastern University late one winter afternoon. She was 21, a senior, and had to make what seemed like the most important decision of her life, and she had little time left to make it. She had been heavily involved in my behavioral neuroscience research laboratory as an undergraduate research assistant. I knew her well. I always thought of her as a nice kid and a gifted student. At that moment, she was under tremendous pressure.

It is not accurate to say Mariko was my student and leave it at that. Northeastern University has a cooperative education program where students can take a six-month full-time work period interspersed with full-time study, and do that three times in a five-year undergraduate degree program. Mariko did it all, and while she started working in my laboratory group as a freshman volunteer, her first cooperative education experience was at Boston University Medical School. There she worked on problems of neural differentiation, that is, how cells become nerve cells. Her second co-op was with me where she worked on research studying the way the nerve cells in the brains of laboratory animals change with cocaine exposure. Her third co-op was at Children's Hospital at Harvard Medical School, with a professor friend of mine from the days when I was an assistant professor in Harvard's psychology department. There she worked on neural regeneration. Each of these experiences resulted in a scientific paper. Mariko had also studied abroad in Australia, and even did some neuroscience research there.

This rich pattern of full-time lab work that alternated and intertwined with class-based study and part-time volunteer lab work led to her phenomenal growth as a student and a researcher. All of her professors saw it, and it was fascinating that she seemed not to. But that day, she was forced to confront what she had become—one of the best students in America—and decide between her admission offers to Stanford and Harvard medical schools. And she was out of time.

To a casual observer, Mariko's embarrassment of riches was a win-win situation. But she reminded me of an illustration in one of my old psychology textbooks of a donkey standing exactly between two delectable bales of hay. Lightning bolts are shooting out of its head, while the donkey wears a distressed expression on its face. As I remember, the caption read, "Approach-approach conflict can be stressful, too." Indeed, over the few weeks leading up to her medical school decision, I actually felt sorry for Mariko for the stress she was under, even as I was enormously proud of her for earning the choice between two highly positive alternatives.

Adding to the pressure was the fact that she had been admitted into nearly every medical school to which she applied. Mariko had exceeded everyone's expectations, including her own. Students outside the Ivy League were not supposed to achieve such heights. A few years later, when Mariko was at Stanford Medical School, she flattered me by saying, "Jim took a dumb girl from western Massachusetts and got her into the best medical schools in America." Nice words, but of course Mariko did it herself; she was a good student who really developed herself in college. I believe that experiential education helped her to do that.

I believe it can help everyone. You see, Mariko was not alone. I had passing through my laboratory many undergraduate students who thought of themselves as having good but ordinary levels of student talent. Just like me when I was their age, they did not get into an Ivy League undergraduate school. But they achieved beyond their expectations at Northeastern. In the last six years before I left Northeastern University in 2008, those laboratory undergraduates were admitted into top medical schools: one, who actually preceded Mariko, into Stanford; two into Yale; one into NYU; and one into the University of Pennsylvania's veterinary program. The same thing happened with another set of lab students who went on to prestigious PhD programs in neuroscience, receiving generous fellowships from Harvard, MIT, UCSD, and so on. Success was in the air, or maybe in the water, in that laboratory. Just as Mariko had grown at Northeastern, I could see others grow from their experiences, their success evident in their faces and in their increased efforts as they realized they were getting somewhere.

Some people thought I was able to create this success because I was the laboratory director. I did not. I was in the laboratory less and less at that point, as I had become dean of the College of Arts and Sciences. To me, the key factor was that the laboratory was a team. Every person, from professor to graduate student, to undergraduate to technician, brought their best efforts to support that team. I was the principal investigator, true—the official leader—but the lab belonged to all of us. We were like a family that owned the corner grocery store in a small town. We knew we had to work together, and we inspired one another.

At night or on weekends, while many of their peers were studying, socializing, or goofing off, my undergraduates were often in the lab working on experiments. Without my asking, they sometimes ran experiments over holidays. I could see when they were working, if only from the times they sent me text messages asking for the location of some supplies, or e-mails wondering whether they should re-run a procedure that had a result that seemed a little screwy. We all seemed to be having fun; I know that I had a blast. We all grew together. It was work, but it did not feel burdensome.

A Story of an Institution that Transformed Itself

Experiential learning has also played a key role in transforming a university at which I served for 22 years, at which I had a front-row seat to watching and helping.

For a large, private university, Northeastern is somewhat of an anomaly. Most of Boston's major colleges and universities are ivory towers steeped in traditional pedagogies of the library and lecture hall. Northeastern specializes in cooperative education, a style that combines carefully selected and designed work experiences with standard classroom and lab courses. It has done so for over 100 years, following the University of Cincinnati, one of the founding schools of the cooperative-education approach.

At the beginning of my time as dean, I attended a retreat for Northeastern's top administrators, with our president, Richard Freeland, who was also new to the job. He had us read in advance Jim Collins' book on how businesses improve, *Good to Great: Why Some Companies Make the Leap... And Others Don't.* At the time, Northeastern was rated by *US News & World Report* as a third-tier school in America, about 165 on the list of major national universities. Freeland made a quiet call to arms, telling us that with the coming competition in American higher education, as he saw it, Northeastern would be better off it were ranked in the top 100. As his leadership team, we agreed that we could make things better.

To be honest, there was another factor at work. Northeastern had just come through a painful period of campus budget cuts, and it was rough despite able leadership by the previous president. The cuts stemmed from a demographic dip in the college-age population that led the other Boston-area colleges to take more students from their waiting lists. Our problem was that many of those students would have been ours, and we had no real waiting list. Our freshman class size plummeted in one year from about 4,500 to 2,700 students. As a private university, we had few options when our revenue coffers ran dry. We had no state government to back us up. The endowment was not large. That year, we fired well over 100 people because we simply couldn't afford to pay their salaries. We cut back on everything else, too, to live within a budget and the new reality of a smaller freshman class. Just about the time we had gotten used to these changes, stability returned, and President Freeland arrived. Now he wanted us to get better. We all agreed that we wanted never to repeat the trauma of downsizing. To be less vulnerable, we wanted to have a healthy waiting list and a better national ranking. We decided to pursue those goals by promoting both our traditional academic excellence and our signature and distinctive program of cooperative education.

The college of arts and sciences I was leading had also come to the same basic conclusion of pursuing a program of experiential education. In fact, a few years earlier, when I was the associate dean of the College of Arts and Sciences under then-dean Robert Lowndes, we had developed and passed a plan to require experiential education of all students by the year 2000. We designed the college requirement around Northeastern's model of cooperative education, but added features of service-learning, undergraduate research, and study abroad that better suited a liberal arts and sciences college rather than a professional school. Also, we reasoned that having more things for a student to do would more easily allow the students to complete the new requirement. What I did not know at the time or see then as clearly as I see now, was that we were helping to invent the rich panoply of activities that we now call experiential education.

Freeland's plan to raise the university's reputation and attract more students would need a marketing component. We settled on a branding campaign. The campaign chose the key phrases of *higher education* and *richer experience*, which were advertised in signs on campus and on billboards in nearby cities. The ideas appeared in picture form as well. For example, one billboard showed a photograph of student raising his hand in class next to another photograph of the same student hand-signaling a bid at the stock exchange. Another poster featured a student holding one leg of a human skeleton in a classroom, with the professor looking on from behind, while the adjacent scene showed the same student on a football field holding the leg of a player with the coach standing behind him. My favorite poster showed a photograph of a professor at the blackboard lecturing to a class. A female student sat in the front row, her blond hair spilling out from under a baseball cap. In the picture beside it, the curve the professor was drawing on the chalkboard continued as the vapor trail of a space shuttle blasting off across the sky. In that second scene, the blond female student's baseball cap displayed the logo of an aerospace company that worked with NASA. We ended up not using that one after the Challenger space shuttle explosion, but I thought it made the connection particularly well between classroom learning and experience.

The branding campaign was a major effort. Northeastern's enrollment management office identified cities outside the Boston region where we had alumni. With the development staff, they coordinated the posting of advertising with alumni events. Such campaign tactics were smart, but the bottom line, to me, was that we had something good to sell: a wide and deep dedication to a different model of education combining intensive, experience-based learning with academic scholarship in the classroom.

Northeastern made other changes, too, transforming itself from a commuter school with only a few dormitories into a largely residential school that housed most, if not all, students who wanted to live on campus. As new residence halls and parking garages went up, the open spaces in between were transformed and landscaped. The university changed its feel from parking lot to park.

The real driver of success, I believe, was selling the cooperative education program. I saw that especially in the College of Arts and Sciences, where it was unusual, as most cooperative education programs were in professional schools. At student recruitment events, we boasted that 70 percent of our students received job offers, either at graduation or in the summer just afterward, and that many of those job offers were from co-op employers or other companies in the same industry. We also noted that many of our graduates were declining those job offers to attend medical, law, business, engineering, or other graduate schools. It seemed to me to be powerful stuff for prospective applicants—and it showed in the results.

Gradually at first, Northeastern's applicant pool grew larger. The yield of accepted students began to get stronger and we started to notice more and more students choosing us over what were then better ranked schools, like Boston University. The applicant pool kept growing.

During that time, I was appointed dean, and at just at the college I led, applications for 1,100 freshman places climbed from about 5,000 to 15,000. The average SAT scores of the incoming freshman class rose by about 250 points. Our retention of students improved, too, and the number of students who graduated with a major in one of the departments or programs in arts and sciences grew from about 3,700 to 6,800 students. The growing size made the College of Arts and Sciences a strong revenue generator for the university, generating millions of dollars each year beyond what was targeted for us. That fact was a great relief to those of us who remembered the budget-cut days.

When I became dean, one of the college's professors told me that he always thought the job of the dean's office was to make his regular classes more like his honors classes. When I stepped down as dean, he stopped by my office and said we had succeeded. He was incredulous and happy. His everyday classes felt to him like the honors classes of old. I saw it too. Working with the departments, I found that our academic success was making it easier to recruit professors who had strong research backgrounds. Faculty members wanted to be part of an institution with a reputation that was on its way up.

In November 2010, after I left Northeastern, *The Chronicle of Higher Education* wrote an article on institutions that sought to improve their reputations. It cited Northeastern, along with USC, Boston University, NYU, and Drexel, as examples of institutions that had done it. By then, Northeastern was booking one of the largest applicant pools of all private universities in America. Moving from a ranking that would charitably be called "undistinguished" to being discussed as a model of achievement was a heady ride.

To be clear, I'm not claiming that the College of Arts and Sciences was wholly responsible for Northeastern's ascent, but I have no doubt that it contributed. Likewise, I cannot prove that cooperative education and the larger experiential education program was responsible for this bright chapter of Northeastern's story. As a scientist, I know that we did not do a random-assignment experiment, or even have a control group of a comparable university that made similar improvements but without an experiential-learning program. But as an administrator, I believe that experiential education was central to Northeastern's rise. As a dean and a professor who employed undergraduate research students, I saw how it contributed to the growth of our students. Our successful students like Mariko could attest to the importance of experiential education to their success, and they did. In fact, they became the best promoters of Northeastern. The best promotion is word of mouth from trusted peers, and Northeastern had it with students and even with professors whom we sought to recruit.

My Story

When I decided to write this book, I made a number of decisions. The first one was writing style. When I began my graduate training in neuroscience, I had to read a mountain of technical scientific literature that other scientists knew and followed every day. I also had to learn how to write for them. They were the professors on my graduate committees, editors at the journals in which I needed to publish, and reviewers of my grant applications for the necessary funding to do the research. The value in that community was on being succinct, precise, and utterly clear to the expert. In science, we rarely explained the exact path we took to get to the final design of the experiment. That was not to be deceptive. It was done to save words. Scientists are busy people. At scientific meetings and particularly after the conference day at dinners and in the bars with friends we would discuss how many ways we tried a technique to make it work before we found the right method. The important thing in writing was clarity.

I really liked the stripped-down, scientific writing style and I thought it helped me as an administrator to cut through any crap and get to the point. But I wanted broad accessibility in this book, so I took a stiff drink and decided to do something simple. I decided I would just talk to you, the reader, as though you were a dear, old friend from outside the field and we were having a nice conversation over dinner, a very long conversation at that.

Another decision I made long ago was to value collaboration, particularly with those who are coming up in the growth process. Despite competition between laboratories in science, I found that I could do well as a researcher by working with students as colleagues and with colleagues as friends. I have tried to apply this same thinking to my time in university administration and it seems to work. People like it, they work hard, and they bring forward their best ideas. There are even business advice books written on this kind of leadership approach, such as in Jim Collins' *Good to Great*.

So how does that decision to collaborate apply to our "dinner conversation" and this book? As mentioned in the preface, this book is connected to a blog, The Other Lobe (www.otherlobe.com), which I began writing in February 2009, and in which almost every blog post is co-authored. As discussed in the preface, that collaborative effort was supplemented by a private website where a sub-set of us discussed book chapters as they emerged. I am in the debt of all of those people, who really shaped my thinking and my writing.

Finally, I need to tell you that I am an expert in basic neuroscience. I spent my professorial life studying reward and motivational brain circuits in laboratory rats. My lab worked on cocaine addiction, specifically on gene expression changes in relevant brain regions and behavioral cues. I sometimes called us "behavior-pharmaco-neuroanatomists," a term I joyfully took from one of my dearest friends and a very successful neuroscientist, Ann Kelley, who unfortunately for us all died from colon cancer before her time. I had fantastic students, got enough funding to survive, loved my teaching, and made a nice life as a professor. I had the privilege of teaching at some great institutions, including the University of Pennsylvania, where I was trained, and later at Harvard University as a young assistant and then associate professor of psychology. In addition, I had a very good, long run as a researcher at Northeastern University.

When I moved to be provost at Queens College in 2009, I stopped the lab. My DEA drug license to buy cocaine lapsed. I now have no machines to maintain and no need to apply for grants to support my students and the technicians. But I still read and attend scientific meetings. With some funding I continue to receive from a foundation for which I do reviews, I still try to involve undergraduates in a lab-like experience of writing the blog. Sometimes I joke that, as an administrator, now I do experiments on institutions and instead of rats. The small point here is that I really do see the organization of the university as if it were like a brain. Where I formerly had a brain atlas, I now have an organization chart. Where I would have applied neuroscience methods to alter the structure and function of the brain, I now work with colleagues to change the college or university with new programs or strategic plans and see if it makes things better.

Finally, I am now writing outside my area of professorial expertise, trying to figure out how books like Maclolm Gladwell's *Blink* or David Eagleman's *Incognito* or Michael Gazzaniga's *Who's in Charge* or Daniel Pink's *Drive* or Jonathan Haidt's *The Happiness Hypothesis* or Daniel Kahneman's *Thinking Fast and Slow* or Joshua Greene's *Moral Tribes* could be applied to programs of experiential education in colleges and universities. As we will discuss in a subsequent chapter, I believe that the fMRI machine is letting us all look into the workings of the brain as it operates and makes decisions, and that actually helps our thinking here. Neuroscience is expanding to influence other fields, like neuroeconomics. Please know that we are taking general lessons from this scientific literature. I am not proposing to brain scan a student before and after an internship, at least not yet.

Then there are the whole areas of higher-education research, such as high-impact practices and many others, that are outside my research field. So, I will leave them to others. I mean no disrespect; all of this work is important and much of it is accessible online, but my goal here is to construct a persuasive argument that experiential education is important to higher education, and that it fits with the way the brain works — at a very basic level it is natural.

I want to make one more very personal point. Experiential education got me started in my career. I had a lab experience in the summer between my junior and senior years when one of my Ursinus College professors, George Sharp, suggested I try it. I went to the University of Pennsylvania where professor Randy Gallistel took a chance on me that summer, and later as his PhD student. My father was a life mentor, but not a field mentor — at least not at that point. Later, we did write a book together, *The Neurobiology of Motivation and Reward* (1985).

My experiences in Gallistel's laboratory that first summer filled me with a passion that, until that time, I really had only felt about surfing. Even my mother commented on the change, an important confirmation of the path on which Professor Sharp had set me. Despite having a father in the field, until then, I had no idea how incredibly cool the brain was or what I could do academically with that interest. I never thought I could go to graduate school at the University of Pennsylvania, much less get an assistant professorship at Harvard University. I have seen this uncertainty about career choice in my students and I have watched them overcome it in my laboratory by doing research with us. As I said above, I have seen them exceed their expectations, just as I did with mine.

Conclusion

Why is all of this personal stuff worth mentioning in the beginning of a book on experiential education?

Emotions are important and, of course, they are personal. As you will see, we think with them and with a vast part of our computational brain, of which neuroscientists suggest we are largely unaware. Yet, higher education often seems to ignore this kind of gut-level reasoning in the structure of college education, with its dominant one-to-many classroom instruction style and its emphasis on a fair, transparent process in curriculum requirements, course syllabi, and testing. Online learning can help reach many, but it can be less personal than going to class and sitting with peers. Universities need to be efficient and use some large classes, but doing so can also earn us the ivory-tower reputation. When in life did an employee ever get asked a multiple-choice question? Life is an essay. When is life fair? Life does not follow a syllabus. Is it any wonder that the business community complains our students are well trained intellectually but not work-ready? Is it any wonder that some of our students are disengaged?

So, how do we help? There are always many ways to solve a problem. I will explore one way, and that does not begin by throwing out academics as we know it. It begins by adding some learning from experience, particularly with partners from outside the academy. If the College of Arts and Sciences at Northeastern University can do it and make great strides in its ranking and applicant pool, others can too.

Most colleges and universities already do some experiential education through community service or study abroad or undergraduate research with faculty, and more are doing it every year. But do they leverage those important experiences with reflection and mentoring? Do they connect it to the academic programs of instruction? Do they work with industry, either for-profit or non-profit? Do they understand that experiential education touches a different part of the student's mind than classical academic education? Do they know that by combining the academic facts and theories with direct personal experience, they can educate the whole student?

Is what I just said right? I wrote this book so you could decide.

CHAPTER 2:

Experiential Education:
A Few Basic Definitions

Experiential education is a term that really defines itself[1]. In the context of higher education, it is an organized, academically integrated way to learn from experiences outside the classroom, such as working at a job. Learning while working has a long tradition all over the world and in many forms. It has long existed in the trades, where students apprenticed themselves to a practitioner and learned by doing. Many professions require some kind of internship or residency before a student can practice them. How else, for example, would one learn surgery? Simulators may someday be as good preparation for medicine as they are today for flying an airplane. Until then, one cannot be a medical doctor without working at the elbow of an experienced practitioner — as has been true for centuries.

---

1 Although the words themselves really do define the concept, experiential education has its intellectual basis in work of Brian Kolb in the 1980s, e.g. Kolb, B. (1984). *Experiential Learning: Experience as the Source of Learning and Development*. Upper Saddle River, NJ: Prentice Hall, Inc. Other authors, too numerous to name, have used also the term.

Experiential education at a university can take many forms, covering a spectrum of authenticity and level of commitment. Here are the forms that are most popular today:

Cooperative Education: A full-time, paid, semester-long internship in a chosen profession is the most serious and intense type of experiential learning—the "most real" version of the real world. A key feature of an internship is that they can be repeated, so the student may have multiple experiences, often in similar organizations or related industries. The university is deeply involved in setting up and organizing the internship, making the experience much more likely to fit with the student's field of study than if it were not involved.

When an employer pays the student they are likely to better utilize them for real work, typically making the student experience better. From the company perspective and aside from basic fairness and potential legal issues, having the student do real work more deeply allows the company to get to know a potential future employee. As some have said, an internship is the ultimate job interview.

Part-Time or Shorter-Term Internship: Sometimes a student is not available for an entire semester but can spare a summer break or a short winter or spring term. He or she may only want to work part-time while attending classes. The best part-time internships can provide an immersion into the work site so the student almost forgets he is in college. Some weaker part-time internships fall short of a rich experience, leaving the student feeling that the time was wasted, particularly if they are unpaid.[2] It is the university's job to ensure that internships that are part-time are useful to the student's college development, legitimate, safe, and, comply with fair labor practice laws. An internship that is merely convenient and fits the student's schedule is not worthwhile if it is not a positive learning experience that is useful to his or her career.

---

2 The book *Intern Nation* by Ross Perlin in 2012 tells of the downside of internships motivated by industry's desire for low-cost labor and university's desires to promote that they have internship programs.

Job Shadowing and Field Experience: Even briefer workplace experiences can be important and may require only a small institutional commitment to organize. In job shadowing, a student may meet with a professional for only a few hours or half-day, several times a term. A university that invests a little more effort can turn those individual experiences into group activities. For example, a team of students might visit a work site for an hour or two to meet with managers, observe, and ask questions. Such activities can be scheduled during the academic year or on a short term or spring break, which most colleges already use for student travel or service opportunities.

Entrepreneurship: Some students work with alumni or industry mentors on entrepreneurial projects for a concentrated period. In some cases the experiences are for academic credit and in others for just the experience. Entrepreneurship activities have grown as an interest and such projects can open a student's eyes to career possibilities. They also are a great way for a university to cultivate alumni relationships more deeply than by simply asking for an annual gift. My current institution at the University at Albany is embarking on a broad entrepreneurship project for many students this year under a major grant from the Blackstone Foundation.[3]

Study Abroad: Sending students abroad to take courses in a foreign country provides a completely different experience, moving them out of their national cultures and sometimes languages. Students who leave those comfort zones seem to learn more rapidly than on the home campus. Even when goofing off, they get to know the new culture in a way that is impossible from the home country. At the same time, they gain a new perspective on their own country. The further that students go outside their comfort zone, the better—as long as they can adapt to it. Again, the student's home university has to help make the challenge a good one.

Faculty-Led Trips Abroad: A university faculty member may take students on trip abroad combined with a course. Students traveling in a

---

3 https://www.blackstonelaunchpad.org

group tend to reflect together on their experiences in the foreign country, in a way that is both intensive and natural. As will be discussed later, reflection leverages experience-based learning powerfully, contributing both to the academic and career development of the student. And having a faculty member teach the course assures the university that it will be on par with its on-campus courses. A professor may provide advice to students while abroad, and then follow-up on the return to campus, by engaging students in other related courses or research.

Service and Service-Learning: Efforts to serve the community can be opportunities for students to serve and to learn. Community service has the added benefit of burnishing the university's reputation for public engagement. Service-learning is designed specifically to intersect with a course of study, most beneficially in the field of a student's major. Students can see "in the wild" the principles discussed in the classroom—causes of urban homelessness, for example, or the value of a new well to a village that lacked access to clean water. At its finest, service-learning happens within an academic course; the service provides a "lab," much as the lab component for a chemistry course. The service-learning lab is just further afield and perhaps run by another organization.

Undergraduate Research: Most college and university faculty members are not just teachers; they are also scholars. That second role can create opportunities for undergraduates to assist in scholarly work. After all, a college junior or senior is barely younger than the graduate students who are often paid as research assistants. For the past two decades, undergraduate research has been all the rage on campuses in America. But barriers exist: Students can find their professors intimidating and often do not know where to begin contacting them. Professors too can be at sea about supervising undergraduates, or worry they will take time away from faculty scholarship. Faculty members who have been exposed to other faculty members involved in undergraduate research often come around to see it as enjoyable, productive to them, and a very high form of teaching their discipline. When successful, undergraduate research can create a positive bond between faculty member and student. And the student knows just where to turn for a recommendation letter from a professor.

Combinations: Many types of experiential learning can be combined, sometimes in unexpected ways. A service-learning project can be set up overseas. A partner company might agree to start a learning co-op in its research laboratory. A faculty member can take a student to search historical archives in Moscow or to dig at archaeological sites in Africa.

Students are good at dreaming up combinations, but the university can add organization to students' creativity. The goal should be to encourage students to do their own thinking and networking, after they first have developed a logical path of experiential education to focus their energies and frame their proposals.

Good work may lead to unexpected synergies. I had an undergraduate research student who spent a term working at a European neuroscience institute. He arranged the co-op himself when I took him to a Society for Neuroscience meeting to present the undergraduate research he had done with me. When he returned from Europe, he brought back to the laboratory a technique that was unknown to us. While we did not actually implement that technique, the student has since published a paper with me. More importantly, his scientific maturity helped him get into graduate school and earn his PhD in neuroscience at Harvard Medical School.

Innovations: By being open to creative combinations of experiential education, students and the university may be truly innovative. For example, at Queens College CUNY, where I was provost for a while, students from diverse populations have been engaging in profound conversations that focus on increasing understanding between groups that may be historically antagonistic. The college's Center for Ethnic, Racial, and Religious Understanding[4], has a stated goal to "produce students trained in conflict

4 http://www.cerru.org/

mitigation who possess the ability to reach across cultural divides and are motivated by their positive experiences to pursue social change."

What conflicts are suited to this training? A first thought might be the Arab-Israeli conflict, but a moment's reflection turns up dozens of ethnic, racial, and national divides that have populations at each other's throats. I wonder whether this type of experience should be added to the list of experiential education forms.

Many other forms may be waiting to be discovered—some organized by students, some involving professors, some partnering with outside organizations. The development of experiential education, at this point in its history, should be open-ended. I wonder how these experiences might be used to help improve college education for all but particularly for underserved populations.

But there are hallmarks of quality that anyone involved with experiential education should consider. For example, if activities are to be a formal part of the university education, there must be some sort of evaluation. Otherwise, how would you know if a program is any good and really does lead to enhanced learning?

There are other questions, too. What is the role of business in designing and implementing such programs within the university? Do we let the marketplace just run those programs and evaluate after? We are preparing many of our students for that workplace. Also, businesses often have money and technology that universities lack: Can we make them partners in educating students, as long as we keep our mission clear? Finally, what if a business goes into the business of helping create internships? One such new company, iQ4[5], creates virtual projects with industry that function like small internships, except everything is on a laptop or mobile device. As of this writing, they are working with schools at CUNY and SUNY on insider threat in cybersecurity.

---

5 http://www.iq4.com

A whole set of other questions arise from a deeper level: the nature of the human brain. As the next few chapters will reveal, the most profound argument for experiential education is that the brain may learn differently when engaged in real-world experience than in the contrived activities of standard classroom. If that is so, a university that offers only traditional classes, as good as they may be, is shortchanging its students, educating just part of them. If that is so, experiential education may be a key to meeting many of the criticisms that are raised about higher education today.

The Brain

❖

CHAPTER 3:

What Every Citizen Needs to Know About the Brain

My goal in this chapter is to introduce you to the few basic concepts about the brain that will help you to appreciate the rest of the book. Not to worry. I have done a lot of neuroscience teaching to general student populations in my career and everyone survives, even those with no science background. However, if you have had a basic neuroscience class or a neuroscience-focused psychology class, this chapter may be more of a partial review. I still suggest that you skim it anyway just to see what aspects of this vast field of neuroscience are most relevant to experiential education. I also encourage the novice reader to follow up with a little online research. But beware, this field is so fascinating that one could get sucked into it and spend considerable time there. I was so drawn to the field, I made it a career.

A Myth of Neuroscience

There are a lot of myths in neuroscience. One of them, which used to drive me crazy in my first years of teaching at Harvard, goes like this: "Professor: I hear we only use 10 percent of our brain. Is that true?" I always wanted to say in my best whiny voice, "How would I know? The brain has no operating manual like your phone or your computer because we did not make it." But that would have been rude. Instead, I always tried to be patient and explain that although there is much about the brain we do understand, there is so much that we do not. Why is this so?

The first reason is that the brain has a large number of pieces and they are connected together in very complex ways. Consider that in the few pounds of soft gelatinous brain material safely carried inside a hard human skull, there are about 100 billion microscopic nerve cells, also called neurons. To put this number in some scale, the number of neurons in your head is about fourteen times larger than the current number of humans on the planet earth. And, like humans, each neuron can interact with thousands of its peers. The analogy is useful because even in a modern world with all of its available information, social media, and analysis, we accept the fact that no one can accurately predict the future behavior of human society, even in important areas such as major economic bubbles or political shifts in national leadership or rapidly emerging conflicts between groups and even countries. Maybe we should not be surprised that no one really understands how neurons work together to create the complex behaviors that we humans so effortlessly display all the time.

The second challenge to understanding the brain is that its pieces, the neurons, are microscopic, so we are just starting to figure them out. For example, we have known for my lifetime that neurons connect to each other across small gaps called synapses, that they use very small amounts of specific chemicals called neurotransmitters to communicate across these synapses, and that these neurotransmitters have powerful effects on the next neuron in the sequence. But it is much more complicated than that. The neurotransmitters interact and alter each other's function by altering the biochemistry of the cell, even it gene expression. Even the surrounding glia cells, which I was first taught as a graduate student were thought to merely bring in nutrients and take out waste, can interact with the process of neurotransmission.

Perhaps the most powerful process that enhances the computational power of neural circuits is found in dendritic spines. A dendrite is one of a neuron's many very small branches that receive inputs, and now we know that each dendrite can have thousands of spines. A whole neuron might have hundreds of thousands of spines, greatly enhancing the computational possibilities that lie in the connections between neurons. But what really floors me is that dendritic spines seem to be coming and going on the surface of the dendrite. In enriched environments that drive inputs to these neurons, the dendritic spines increase. They swell up and make contact with the incoming neuron's synaptic input. When the activity dies down, some of them go away. The brain's neurons are literally alive with physical movement at this tiny microscopic level. When we learn something, we literally reshape the cellular architecture of our brains.

Today, we call these and other ways in which neurons and other components of the brain's cellular structure touch each other the *connectome* to emphasize the super-complex circuits that encode who we are now. The genes may have started us out in life, but our experiences have changed and enriched the brain's structure, making us who we are today. It is just staggering how many possibilities there are for such connections in the brain. But maybe it has to be that way, considering how smart we are. Lyall Watson, the South African biologist and author, put it well in an often-quoted statement, "If the brain were so simple we could understand it, we would be so simple we couldn't."

With all of these connections, it may not be so surprising that the brain has an amazing capacity for information storage. For example, we all use a sophisticated language that we learned as children. We easily recognize so many faces from many viewing angles, and we store vivid memories of some events even from long ago. In this way, the brain does seem like a computer. But even here, the brain is doing something different. As the author of the 2008 book *Kluge*, Gary Marcus[1], discusses, the brain does not use a computer-like postal-address form of memory, where each memory is given a fixed location in the machine's architecture like the postal address of a house on a street. Instead, the brain seems to use a more context-dependent system, and so is subject to errors and imperfections that we do not expect from computers. Even so, no computer has yet been made that comes close to the operations of our brain in thinking and in using its memories to grow and become the individual people we are. One of the saddest syndromes in neurology today is Alzheimer's disease, which causes the memories and complex rational thinking to fade away as the disease progresses, stealing much of the essence of the person.

The Brain Works by Different Rules than a Computer

Since the computer is such a strong analogy for the brain, I feel I have to push back on this topic here to indicate what is critically different about brains. And I prefer to do it with a story. The story starts when I had just earned my PhD degree, was a postdoctoral fellow at the University of Pennsylvania Medical School, and thought I was finally done with all the courses I would ever take for the rest of my life. But I signed up to take an informal course that was taught by one of the anatomy professors, who was just getting into small personal computers, which were new at the time. As I remember, the course was called "The Psychobiology of the Southwest Technical Products 6800 Microprocessor System." He wanted us to

---

1 Gary Marcus, *Kluge: The Haphazard Evolution of the Human Mind*, Houghton Mifflin: New York, NY, 2008.

treat that chip as a tiny brain and study its central processing unit (CPU) architecture the way a neuroscientist would. We learned about the CPU's registers, how it moved the data around, and did its basic computations.

The final exam in the course was to use our knowledge of the structure of the CPU and its registers to write in machine code a simple program that would find the maximum and minimum of a list of numbers. Machine code is very basic, as it is one step away from the one's and zero's that the CPU actually uses to operate. As an aside, we wrote the program on the lab's PDP-11 microcomputer, a big machine at the time made by the Digital Equipment Corporation, now out of business. Today, the PDP-11 is a museum piece and the CPU in your cell phone or mobile device has more computing power. But at the time, anatomy students and postdoctoral fellows alike would work on it late in the day. Occasionally at night, well after the professors had gone home, we would play "Adventure," a text-based, cave-navigation, treasure-hunting game popular in the late 1970s.

All of these devices, from my modern laptop to the old chip that I studied in that course, share a common feature. Every CPU does its processing one step at a time, and every computer has a built-in clock that sequences the CPU in executing those steps. The program I wrote was really a list of steps for the CPU to execute. It does not matter whether the CPU is reading data from memory locations, transferring the data to the central processer, making calculations, and so on. It does every step one at a time, just very fast.

The brain does not work this way. There is no rigid central clock and no step-by-step processing in neural circuits. Even the biochemistry inside a neuron is not organized one step at a time with a rigid central clock. Each neuron's internal chemical structure and its role in computations in a circuit are done on their own time, in response to input from other neurons and other sources. With all of these processes happening at once, from the perspective of an orderly computer program, like even the small one I wrote, it is amazing that the brain works at all.

Where the brain has a great advantage over a computer is in its massively parallel architecture. Now it is true that we do have parallel CPU architecture in modern computers, but nothing like 100 million CPUs – if one considers every neuron to be like a little computer, and I do. That truly incredible parallel processing capacity of all those networked neurons more than makes up for the slow speed of neuron-based computation compared to very fast speed of silicon-based computation in computers. For my whole lifetime, robotics has been promising us robots that can walk on two legs, but none of them are as good as my daughters were when they were three years old. It has been just too big of a computational task to control all of those muscles and joints—but not for the brain of a child.

With all of this discussion of microscopic structure and computational power to store and process information, you might think I had already told you the most important brain concept for this book, but I have not. That comes next.

Brain Areas and Localization of Function

Starting with the idea of neurons in the brain as people on the planet, let's extend that analogy to consider that groups of neurons are like communities, and brain regions are like countries. Let's take as an example the language circuitry in the brain and see how these very basic functions are localized, in most people, to fairly specific brain places.

One part of the brain that has to do with speech production is called Broca's area. One of the earliest parts of the brain to be described scientifically, it was discovered by Paul Broca (1824–1880) after he observed patients who had damage to this brain area. He noticed that they had also lost the power of speech but could understand the speech of others.

Broca's area is classically located at the bottom back of the frontal lobe on the left side. It was not known at the time, but that finding is especially common in right-handed males. If you are a right-handed guy, put your left forefinger on your head, just in front of your left ear. If you have a modest-sized stroke there, the chances are very good that you will never speak again, at least not well. We know today that women and left-handers tend to have a bit more dispersal of speech functions on both sides of the brain and so do a bit better after such a stroke.

What makes this story even more intriguing is that, just a bit farther back, at the top back of the temporal lobe, is a brain area that seems to process language understanding. If a stroke damages Wernicke's area, named after Carl Wernicke (1848–1905), you cannot understand speech, but you can continue to produce it, complete with subject-verb agreement and plurality.

The problem for the patient is that without guidance from Wernicke's area, Broca's area produces speech that is nonsense. Clearly, Broca's production and Wernicke's reception areas are the beginning of a map of the human language circuit and language is much more complicated than this simple picture. This brain cartography is based on assigning behavioral functions to brain areas, just as some human communities are known for certain industries, such as fishing villages or mining towns.

To give a contrast to this simple story of the localization of function in language, let us consider a syndrome that is a bit more mysterious, sensory neglect. People with this syndrome tend to neglect everything on one side of their personal space. These people dress half their bodies. They eat half the food on their plates, unless you turn the plate around for them, and then they will eat the remaining food. If you show them words, one letter at a time, that can be divided, like *baseball,* they are likely to read the word *ball.* In one amazing thought experiment, a neurologist asked such a patient to imagine standing in a specific place in a familiar Italian piazza and to name the surrounding buildings. The patient named all of the buildings on the right and none on the left. Then the neurologist asked the patient to walk in his mind to the other side of the piazza, turn around, and name the buildings. Again, he named all the ones on his right and none on the left. The interesting thing was that the two sets of buildings so named did not overlap. The "neglect of the left" syndrome in this patient applied not only to stimuli received through the senses, but it also applied to the mental structure of that piazza in his mind. The point of the neglect story is that some syndromes seem simple at the outset, but they do not yield to easy understanding. The state of modern neuroscience is that some very important ideas are still emerging; I will try to tell you where we know more and where we know less in the areas we are considering in this book.

Neurologist Oliver Sacks' wonderfully titled bestseller, *The Man Who Mistook His Wife for a Hat*,[2] raises an intriguing question. Why a hat? The man who mistook his wife for her sister would be much more understandable. We have much to learn about how the circuits of the brain work. The mystery here is more than just brain cells. Fortunately, we have modern brain scanning machines, which I will discuss in the next chapter. I think they will help if we are clever enough to use them well. The immense challenge will be to link our understanding of the complexity of behavior with the complexity of brain function. This fascinating and complex work will require careful thinking on both sides of the issue. But the story that unfolds over the next few decades may be one of the most interesting and challenging to our ideas of who we are and how we work as human minds, not to mention as college students seeking an education.

Levels of Function in the Brain

The complexities of the brain can seem overwhelming to me and perhaps to you. In such a case, I look for something basic, something fundamental upon which I can mentally stand to drive my thinking. A fundamental idea in neuroscience is that the brain is organized in levels, starting with the most

---

2 Oliver Sacks, *The Man Who Mistook His Wife For A Hat: And Other Clinical Tales*, Touchstone, 1998.

basic at the bottom and going to the most sophisticated at the top. Some have compared this arrangement to the well-defined military hierarchy where low-level soldiers know little of the strategy of war that the high-level generals plan. In reverse, the generals are typically not as aware as their soldiers of what the soldiers experience every day.

Scientists think that the brain's hierarchical arrangement comes from its evolutionary history. As a human develops, starting in the womb, it moves from brain mechanisms that control the most fundamental behaviors, such as swallowing, to more and more sophisticated behaviors. That sequence seems to recreate the fundamental pattern of our evolution as we develop.

Although others theorized about a hierarchical structure earlier, Paul MacLean (1913-2007)[3] formulated a theory in the 1960s that is simple, and therefore useful for this book. He called his structure the *triune brain*, which, not surprisingly, features three levels. The bottom level he called *reptilian* to connote its earlier evolutionary history and concern with basic functions.

MacLean called the top level *neomammalian*, where *neo* means new. That level is sometimes also called the *primate brain*. With its powerful six-layer neocortex, the primate brain handles all the sophisticated cognitive computational tasks of language, face-recognition, mathematics, making art, and so on. It wraps over the older brain and hence gets the term *cortex* or *bark* from the way bark wraps a tree.

What remains in this three-level hierarchical representation is the middle level. MacLean called this portion *paleomammalian*, where *paleo* means old. He also referred to it as the *limbic system*. For our discussion, I will use the *mammalian brain* and the *limbic system* interchangeably. We think of the limbic system as mediating the emotions, but it does much more. The limbic system has fascinated me for my entire scholarly life and it still does. It directed our evolutionary ancestors' actions before the neocortex evolved;

---

3 A good account of Paul MacLean can be found at https://en.wikipedia.org/wiki/Paul_D._MacLean

it made them get up when they were hungry, told them when to stop and eat when they found something good, especially if they had eaten it before with a good outcome. The limbic system put our ancestors to rest to save energy and to stay safe until it was time to again do something important like eat or mate.

Since emotions tend to be viewed as a squishy concept, I have to point out that the control process I have described is quantitative, even mathematical. I can say that because an important discovery in psychology—by B. F. Skinner, a Harvard professor—was of operant behavior and its detailed control by reinforcement. In simple terms, an operant behavior is a voluntary action an animal or human learns to perform to get something desired, such as food when hungry. In this case, food is the reinforcement or the reward for performing the act. Skinner often put laboratory rats in a clear plastic box with a lever sticking out of the wall that the rat could press. When the rat pressed the lever, typically a few times, food was delivered to the box. Sometimes these boxes were called Skinner boxes and they became a common feature of almost every psychology department.

Building on that concept, Richard Herrnstein, one of Skinner's students, who also became a Harvard professor, demonstrated that pigeons, rats, and humans all responded in precisely the same way when tested with a choice between two reinforcements, each with its own lever. The researchers found that subjects would match the vigor of their lever pressing behavior on one lever versus the other lever to the differences in the payoff between the two reinforcements. If one lever gave twice as much reinforcement as the other lever, the subject pressed that lever twice as often as the other lever. Herrnstein called his discovery the *matching law*, which we will return to in more detail in Chapter 6. For now, I want to point out that trade-offs or choices between alternatives, even if unconscious, are highly relevant to a discussion of experiential learning and the mammalian brain.

These choices between alternatives can even exist over time. A person, or even a rat, requires a much larger reward if it is given later so as to not take a smaller reward given now. Otherwise, it will choose the smaller more immediate reward. That behavior is especially clear when the trade-off is between a pleasant and an unpleasant alternative. What parent has not scolded his or her children to turn off the TV set right now and to do their homework so they are ready for school tomorrow? What college student has not regretted partying until all hours last night, when she or he is stepping into the classroom now to take an exam?

We constantly make similar decisions about what to do, when to do it, and the amount of effort to commit to the task. We make these decisions in our limbic system, in our mammalian brain. Sure, we look at our watch and see the hours of study time slipping away while we are at the party for a friend. But how do we decide when the threshold is crossed, the trade-off point is reached, and it is time to leave? I suggest it is the limbic system that makes the call. The mammalian brain has no words. It sends its messages through feelings. The conscious person that is "you" thinks it does the deciding. But this limbic system has its own store of knowledge—enough, many times over, to make the key judgments and most vital decisions of a person's life, like when you feel it is time to leave the party or whether that person you just met is someone you might want to marry.[4]

Unfortunately, colleges and universities generally fail to recognize the educational potential of the mammalian brain in their students. Many institutions see only the negative aspects of it, such as when college students morph into party animals and neglect their studies. As currently structured, higher education and the college classroom generally focus on the conscious facts-and-theories form of knowledge processing that is housed in the neocortex. That focus is perhaps unsurprising, because the neocortex is the part of the brain that talks; it makes up the stories one tells about oneself.[5]

4 David Eagleman, *Incognito: The Secret Lives of the Brain*, Random House: New York, NY, 2011.
5 Michael Gazzaniga, *Who's in Charge*, Ecco: New York, NY, 2011.

But, as we will see, a focus on the neocortex alone is wrong, because it misses so much.

In this chapter, we have seen that the brain is complex and made of tiny pieces organized into circuits that occupy specific areas of the brain and communicate with other regions. The brain circuits and regions are somewhat independent of each other, leading to a massively parallel computational system unlike anything else we know. In addition, several levels of the brain seem to exist, in which higher cognitive and conscious functions are somewhat separated from lower, older motivational and emotional systems. And a great deal of brain activity happens outside of conscious awareness, yet those processes influence our conscious decisions.

Chapter 6 will have much more to say about the mammalian or limbic part of the brain and its involvement in very important but unconscious decision making. But first, we will look at the brain in action, through the remarkable window of the modern brain-scanning machine.

C H A P T E R   4 :

The fMRI Machine: A Neuroscientific Revolution in Our Lifetime.

Something amazing has just happened in the history of science: We humans invented a tool that can look deep inside the living brain and observe its activity, without causing harm. The device is called the functional magnetic resonance imaging (fMRI) machine, and it is touching our society in ways that we are just beginning to see from medical diagnosis and treatment to how we think of ourselves. I believe the fMRI machine has a lot to say about what underlies the effectiveness of experiential education in the college undergraduate, so let me show you something about how it works.

The 19th century physician mentioned in the previous chapter, Paul Broca, had to wait until his patient with the impaired speech died to know what brain area was damaged. That necessary delay was a daunting limitation for a doctor or a scientist, because the patient might happily live a long time, or might unhappily sustain additional brain injury that would obscure the original damage. On top of it all, the brain might be unavailable at the time of death.

In the late 1970s, when I was a postdoctoral fellow, a neurologist friend of mine told me that he had quietly anticipated studying the brain of one of his patients after the man died. My friend had arranged everything with the man's immediate family, but when death came, other relatives wanted to have "Grandpa buried whole," and the brain was suddenly not available for postmortem study. The paper my friend wanted to publish was never written. Today, such work would not be wasted in that way because Grandpa would have had a series of fMRI brain scans while he was alive and the neurologist could have used those images for his paper. Importantly, he also would have had the opportunity to discuss these brain scans with the patient and family as part of the basic medical consultation, improving everyone's understanding of Grandpa's condition.

Though we are discussing brain research on humans in this chapter, I should point out that research on animals has provided a strong foundation for understanding what brain scanners reveal about us humans. For example, one fMRI brain-scan study found that an area of the brain called the nucleus accumbens becomes active when the subject thinks he or she is going to make money. Another study found that the accumbens lights up when subjects looked at pictures of cute baby faces. The authors of each study concluded that the region has something to do with the reward inherent in each of the tasks.

Animal neuroscience has reached the same conclusion about the accumbens through a long history of studies, including some research my laboratory did on the effects of cocaine on laboratory rats. We and other laboratories showed that the rewarding drug cocaine elevates the neurotransmitter dopamine in the accumbens of laboratory rats, and that blocking the dopamine neurotransmitter function in the accumbens markedly weakened the impact of the reward effect of food, or even the highly rewarding direct electrical stimulation of the lateral hypothalamus, another area of the brain. We also showed that rats will learn to press a lever in a Skinner box to self-inject dopamine-stimulating drugs directly into the accumbens, indicating that they find the brain injection rewarding. These basic research results validated the conclusions in humans from fMRI research.

What makes the animal research even more valuable in understanding the human brain is the ability to look at the structure of those brain circuits and the individual nerve cells that compose them. That observation requires a microscope and some way to stain the brain cells, which are otherwise hard to see, even when magnified.

Photographic images of nerve cells are beautiful, like abstract art. When I view slides of well-stained brain tissue through a microscope, I often imagine that I am flying in a small plane, observing the landscape below. Passing over a small city, I imagine I drop lower to see streets or even people. I started this way of imaginary microscope viewing because someone told me that playing this little game would cure the motion sickness that I occasionally felt from moving the slide in the microscope; it worked.

Sometimes I go further in my imaginings. In one of my last laboratory research studies, I used rats exposed to cocaine twice a day for five days and looked at the neurons in the nucleus accumbens. They were stained for a specific protein, one that is associated with changes in gene-expression that occurs right after cocaine treatment. I sometimes pretended that the cells were people who liked Chinese food, and that I could see the landscape where they lived. But this is science, so we counted cells in a small virtual box, and did the same for cells from rats that had not been exposed to drug treatment, and reported the results in a scientific journal. My imaginary microscope viewing technique was left out of the paper.

The Guts of a Brain Scan Machine

If you accept my comparison of the brain to a landscape that has specific features associated with different functions, let me now tell you, in basic terms, how fMRI machines work to reveal that functional landscape in humans without having to take the brain out of the head.

To give a little history, many people think that the story of the modern brain scanner began in Europe in the early 1900s as a mathematical exercise invented by Johann Radon. His basic idea was later adopted by Allan Cormack, a South African physicist who worked at Tufts University in Boston in the 1960s. Cormack developed the first computer methods for calculating an image reconstruction. But it was not until Godfrey Hounsfield built the first brain scanners at EMI Corporation in England[1] in 1972 that the idea caught on and went into widespread medical practice. In 1979, Cormack and Hounsfield received the Nobel Prize for their contributions to medical imaging.

The details of this technology are quite complicated, but here's a simple explanation that captures the essence of it. Imagine you had a profile picture of the lighter face of Johann Radon against a darker background. If you laid a ruler horizontally over that picture and ran a small optical scanner along its edge, you could get a number for the total cumulative brightness along that line. If the line only ran through the dark background above the head, missing the face entirely, the number would be low. If it went through a bit of the background and then through the center of the face the number would be high. If it just crossed the narrow neck, the number would be in between because the neck is smaller than the center of the face.

Now suppose you followed that procedure for a series of closely spaced parallel lines and kept track of the numbers associated with each line. Then further suppose that you tilted the angle of lines slightly and did the whole closely spaced array all over again. Finally, suppose that you

---

1 EMI was already famous for producing the records of the rock group the Beatles.

repeated that process until you had worked your way around to horizontal again. You would have a large set of numbers linked to all the lines you scanned. Once that data was properly entered into a computer, which would work on it with Cormack's algorithms, and you could reconstruct on the computer screen the image of Johann Radon in profile.

You've just pulled off an amazing trick, if you stop and think about it. From a big table of numbers, you have recreated on a computer screen a picture of what you had in front of you. And if you put the parallel lines very close together and had a huge array of numbers and a modern computer, your reconstructed picture could look pretty good. Why is that trick important to this book? If you replace the picture with your three-dimensional head lying in a scanner, and if you replace the first line you drew through the picture with a thin x-ray beam going in the center of your forehead and out the middle of the back of the head, you could get the cumulative x-ray density associated with that x-ray line through the head. Then, if you moved the beam left and right in front of the forehead and collected each x-ray output at the back of the head at each position, and if you then tilted the beam and repeated the back and forth process, and if you did that all the way around the head, you could get the same data as needed to construct a picture on the computer of the head's density to x-rays. Remarkably, this picture appears as if you were looking down, from above, through the top of the head and into your brain. A conventional x-ray would squish everything together, which is why neurologists take front and side x-ray pictures of the head to try to see what is inside. The computer-reconstructed picture we just discussed shows you a slice of the brain, viewed from above, and everything that is inside it as though you had taken the brain out and dissected it.

Of course, the patient is unharmed, as if they just had a conventional x-ray. If a patient came in with a stroke and was having trouble speaking or similar symptoms, the doctors would be able to see the brain damage in the Broca's area at that moment in that slice, without harming the patient.

The x-ray based scan described above is called computerized axial tomography, or a CAT scan, which today has been shortened to CT scan. The CT scan's utility in allowing more direct observation of brain damage was a great advance, but the next machine was even better.

The magnetic resonance imaging (MRI) created images of the brain that were much clearer. There are a few things you should know about how the machine functions. The MRI does not use x-rays. It works by putting a patient in a benign but strong magnetic field. That causes the very atoms that make up everything in our chemistry to align with that magnetic field. Then, the machine uses radio waves to knock the atoms briefly out of alignment, or resonance with the magnetic field. When they come back into alignment, the atoms (and especially hydrogen atoms) emit a signal that the machine can detect.[2]

CT and MRI observations of many human brains underscored what scientists already knew from dissections: that brain anatomy differs slightly among individuals. Let me illustrate with another little story. Back in the day, when I was in postdoctoral training, I had a little job putting whole human brains on the laboratory benches so they would be ready for medical students doing their dissection labs for the neuroanatomy course. Before each lab, I placed the same brain at its assigned bench. In getting to know those examples of the human brain, I could see that the brains varied in their surface structure about as much as human faces. One of them in particular had a long central sulcus in its neocortex, a particular feature that brain anatomists use to divide the frontal lobe of the brain from the one behind it. That brain belonged on lab bench #5. I came to think about it as if it were the face of a lovely friend with a particularly long nose. There was no missing that face. Everyone had as nose, but hers was outstanding! What a central sulcus! That experience made it easier for me to see how humans can be both similar and different in brain structure.

---

2 To get details on MRI, try this website: http://www.cis.rit.edu/htbooks/mri/inside.htm.

With CT or MRI scanners, scientists can see similarities and differences in the interiors of the brain too, which then raise the question of whether those differences relate to function. Fortunately, we have an answer to this question, but to get there, we have to go to the next machine.

For our purposes, an MRI still measures anatomy and is not what we need if we want to answer the question of function. But the clever people who invented these machines found a way of using an MRI to look at function; that is, to observe brain region's dynamic activity produced by doing a behavioral or mental task, not just its static anatomy. The new machine, and our last, is called a *functional magnetic imaging machine* or fMRI.

Here is how it works. Suppose you are sitting in a quiet room and someone starts talking. You listen carefully to understand what they are saying. As discussed in the last chapter, that means your Wernicke's area becomes active. Those active nerve cells use oxygen, and the local blood vessels quickly respond to that need for oxygen by dilating to increase the flow of oxygen-rich blood. The fMRI machine can measure the increased blood flow in the Wernicke's area. It may be a bit awkward as the patient or the research subject does need to have their head in a noisy fMRI scanner machine, but the resulting images show which brain areas were activated by the task. We can finally see what lights up when people are making small movements, perceiving, thinking, feeling, or more.

To be complete, there are other methods to look at brain function. Positron emission tomography (PET), for example, is a machine that generates scans on the basis of labels using a radioactive tracer. That device allows physicians and scientists to chemically tag tracer substances and find where they go in the brain. A magnetoencephalography (MEG) machine uses something called a superconducting quantum interference device to work much faster than an fMRI or PET scanning machine by looking at magnetic fields on the surface or deep within the brain. We could talk a lot about these and other brain scanners, and we probably should. But for now, we will settle for the fMRI, because it is safe, widespread in its usage, and has contributed so much to our understanding of how the brain works.

The fMRI Machine and Decision Making

Perhaps the single greatest discovery made with the fMRI machine that is relevant to this book is that humans process information, decide what to do, and interact with one another in two fundamental ways that end up being conscious and unconscious forms of deciding. This operation is true whether someone is making a purchase in a store or selecting a college major.

In the conscious way of deciding, we know we are doing it. We are aware of the process and the data we have to drive it. The process is deliberative, requires work, and can take time. The conscious process is the platform on which most of the education system is built. It's what students and professors expect from a college lecture: a presentation of facts and theories that transfers knowledge from professor to student. The course syllabus indicates the content, which fits into the student's program of academic study and is likely to show up on the tests.

An economist, particularly an older one, would likely describe the educational system as "rational" and perhaps make a parallel to the rational choice theory that underlies the market economy on which nations are built. However, psychologist Daniel Kahneman, who won a Nobel Prize in economics in 2002, showed there was another factor and that conscious rational behavior and even choice is not the only factor in economic-type decision making.[3]

The other way we think and make decisions is unconscious. Kahneman called this operation "system I" to avoid using loaded terminology as I just did by describing it as *unconscious*. In contrast with

---

3 Daniel Kahneman, *Thinking Fast and Slow*, Farrar, Straus and Giroux, New York, NY, 2011.

conscious thinking, unconscious thinking or decision making is often fast and appears effortless. It leaps to conclusions by inferring patterns, and it is always active. It is hard not to make conclusions from patterns.

At a mention of the word "unconscious," many of us think of the pioneering work of the famous Sigmund Freud and his followers, who made such a splash in the era of Rationalism by showing that we also operate on an unconscious level. To my mind, society has identified Freud too much with clinical psychology and with sex. Today, thanks in part to brain scanners, we can explore the new realm of neuroeconomics. One of the primary questions in this field is how people balance risk and reward in making decisions. In the brain, the balancing act in decision making includes roles for the nucleus accumbens and the insular cortex, and other brain areas. This book is meant to bring those questions about how we decide into our thinking about higher education. Such questions are sorely needed. After all, if rational economic theory can be challenged by research that shows we are both rational and irrational in making economic decisions, why cannot rational educational approaches be challenged by the same logic when students make career-choice decisions?

With fMRI machines, we are poised to see what "lights up" in the brain when we feel empathy, contemplate an altruistic act, or just buy something. While we can find many sources of data from clever behavioral experiments, or from studies of patients with small strokes, tumors, or other accidents that damage specific brain regions, the brain activity measurements of the fMRI machine add such a compelling part of the story that we really do have a revolution happening in how we think of ourselves. You can see the gathering forces of change in the growing number of recent books by neuroscientists, psychologists, and general science writers; I will discuss some of these books in later chapters in the context of specific questions. For now simply scanning the titles is revealing.[4]

---

4   In order of publication date some examples include:
*   Antonio Damasio – *Descartes' Error: Emotion, Reason, and the Human Brain* (2005)
*   Malcolm Gladwell – *Blink* (2005)

- Jonathan Haidt – *The Happiness Hypothesis: Finding Modern Truth in Ancient Wisdom* (2006)
- William Duggan – *Strategic Intuition* (2007)
- Daniel Gilbert – *Stumbling on Happiness* (2007)
- Ori Brafman and Rom Brafman - *Sway: The Irresistible Pull of Irrational Behavior* (2008)
- Gary Marcus – *Kluge: The Haphazard Construction of the Human Mind* (2008)
- Daniel Coyle – *Talent Code: Greatness Isn't Born. It's grown. Here's How* (2009)
- Jonah Lehrer – *How We Decide* (2009)
- Steven Pinker – *How the Mind Works* (2009)
- Dan Ariely – *Predictably Irrational: The Hidden Forces that Shape Our Decisions* (2010)
- Paul Bloom – *How Pleasure Works* (2011)
- Christopher Chabris and Daniel Simmons – *The Invisible Gorilla: How Our Intuitions Deceive Us* (2011)
- Cathy Davidson – *Now You See It* (2011)
- David Eagleman – *Incognito: The Secret Lives of the Brain* (2011)
- Michael Gazzaniga – *Who's In Charge: Free Will and the Science of the Brain* (2011)
- Daniel Kahneman – *Thinking Fast and Slow* (2011)
- Daniel Pink – *Drive: The Surprising Truth About What Motivates Us* (2011)
- Shankar Vedantam – *The Hidden Brain: How Our Unconscious Minds Elect Presidents, Control Markets, Wage Wars, and Save Our Lives* (2011)
- Jonah Lehrer – *Imagine: How Creativity Works* (2012)
- Antonio Damasio – *Self Comes to Mind: Constructing the Conscious Brain* (2012)
- Jonathan Haidt – *The Righteous Mind: Why good people are divided by politics and religion* (2012)
- Bruce Hood – *The Self Illusion: Why There is No You Inside the Head* (2012)
- Steven Pinker – *The Better Angels of Our Nature: Why Violence Has Declined* (2012)
- Daniel Bor – *The Ravenous Brain: How the New Science of Consciousness Explains Our Insatiable Search for Meaning* (2012)
- Joshua Greene – *Moral Tribes: Emotion, Reason, and the Gap Between Us and Them* (2013)
- Leonard Mlodinow - *Subliminal: How Your Unconscious Mind Rules Your Behavior* (2013)
- Richard Thaler - *Misbehaving: The Making of Behavioral Economics* (2015)

CHAPTER 5 :

Rewiring the Adult Brain:
A New Idea in Neuroscience

"Half of what we are going to teach you is wrong, and half of it is right. Our problem is that we don't know which half is which," C. Sidney Burwell, the dean of Harvard Medical School, purportedly said in 1947[1]. Even then, the rate of change of medical knowledge was impressive. Of course, that rate has only accelerated in our time and you will find variations of that quote used by many others today.

How does that idea apply to this book? If you took a college class more than 10 years ago in neuroscience, psychology, or biology, you probably were taught that the brain circuits of adults were hard-wired except for small changes underlying memory formation and skill learning. Based on that dictum, for most of us if you wanted to learn a second

---

1 http://hms.harvard.edu/about-hms/facts-figures/past-deans-faculty-medicine

language without an accent, you really needed to have started as a child, before the end of the brain's critical period for language learning. Once out of childhood, we were pretty much stuck with the brains we had. Education was about learning the facts and theories of accumulated human wisdom—very important but not a fundamental brain re-wiring.

That observation fit well with some solid neuroscience. Scientists David Hubel and Torsten Wiesel received the 1981 Nobel Prize in Physiology or Medicine for their beautiful work on the processing by neurons of visual information in the cortex of the brain. After working out the basic processing mechanisms that underlie the detection of visual features like edges and corners, they also discovered that if, during a critical period of development, a patch was placed over one eye of a research subject, the other eye's neural connections would take over the space in the visual cortex that was originally reserved for the patched eye. If the patch was not removed until after the critical period in development had passed, visual cortical activation no longer occurred when that eye was stimulated. The patched eye effectively became blind. No amount of visual stimulation would restore the circuit; in short, the mature brain appeared to have no *plasticity*, the ability to change.

That eye-patch finding still stands today but is no longer an unqualified, sweeping dogma for the whole brain. For many years, neuroscientists did not really search for evidence of significant plasticity in the adult brain; instead, the field settled for calling the adult brain's structure hard-wired. Now the field is looking, and today we know that it is possible to have a remarkable degree of change in the adult brain even in areas of basic motor control and sensory processing. However, changing the brain's circuits is very hard to do and requires a great deal of effort and engaged, focused practice. It also takes a long time. By contrast, the young brain is remarkable in how effortlessly it establishes the fundamental structures and functional brain circuits based on patterns of neural activity. But that does not mean that we older people who are beyond our childhood are without neuroplasticity, which is good news for higher education.

One obvious place to look for evidence of neuroplasticity is among people of very high achievement. Journalist Malcolm Gladwell famously wrote in *Outliers: The Story of Success* that it takes 10,000 hours of practice to make one an expert in a complex activity—that's so much time that, as he discusses, experts really do become outliers. In 2009, Daniel Coyle, another journalist, wrote a book about outlier performance with a title that is a tipoff as to the role of the brain, *Talent Code: Greatness Isn't Born. It's Grown. Here's How.*

We will consider some of their ideas here in addition to the work of others. But before going to the neuroscience, let us consider one study where the mere perception of being able to reshape the brain's processing mattered a great deal. In 2007, Stanford professor Carol Dweck published the results of an experiment she conducted with Lisa Blackwell and Kali Trzesniewski. They delivered different lectures to two groups of seventh graders. The first group heard a lecture on good study skills. The second group listened to a lecture about brain plasticity that was designed to convince them that they were not stuck with the abilities they had but could change them by working hard. A year later, the second group had done much better in school than the first group.

Perhaps the higher marks were the result of being inspired. That study replicated an earlier study by the same researchers, and is consistent with their broader body of work. They used their findings to start a company to support student learning, MindSet Works Inc., which works with schools. Carol Dweck also wrote a 2007 book on the topic, *Mindset: The New Psychology of Success.*

Belief matters to achievement, as any experienced educator will say. I often wonder how much college students limit their own achievement by not believing that they can excel. No one doubts that different people have different ability sets, but I worry that people accept too easily the preliminary perceptions of their ability. By doing so, they put themselves into an invisible box and turn out just as they expected, instead of becoming high-achieving outliers.

New Neurons in the Adult Brain

Crucial physical evidence that the adult brain can change came, strangely enough, from research on the brains of songbirds. The story of how the birds learn songs has changed the way we think of ourselves. Here is that story.

More than three decades ago, researchers led by Fernando Nottebohm, a neuroscientist and ornithologist at The Rockefeller University, set out to discover how songbirds learned to produce the songs they heard from their parents and memorized as fledglings. Mature songbirds sing to attract a mate, and to sing well enough for successful courtship, they have to practice. An important area in the brain for motor control of a good song is a region that scientists have dubbed the high vocal center, or HVC. Looking at the brains of mature birds, Nottebohm's researchers discovered something astonishing: New neurons were being born in the brain and migrating to the HVC, where they joined the ranks of existing neurons and presumably contributed to the motor-control learning needed to sing a song well. They noticed that a songbird's HVC nucleus varies in size according to the time of year. In spring, when it sings for a mate, the HVC is at its largest. It shrinks during the summer, when the song is least important, then begins to grow again in the fall, as the bird ramps up its singing practice to prepare for spring.

It is true that claims of adult neuroplasticity existed before Nottebohm's work. The field of medicine has known for centuries that peripheral nerves could regrow, and researchers have long searched for ways to promote this neuroplasticity in the central nervous system to treat spinal-cord injury. Yet the scientific and medical communities clung stubbornly to general position that I learned in graduate school and also taught as a young professor—that the neurons a person had at the start of adulthood were all he or she would get, with no replacement. There was also the view, as a secondary position, that if new neurons were somehow introduced into the brain, their arrival would disrupt its complex neuronal circuitry.

Clearly both positions were wrong. Scientists now accept that neurons can be born in the adult brains of all mammals as well as in birds. Research focuses today on such issues as the conditions that produce new neurons, their location in mammals, and their importance to function.

As a brief aside, let me say that this topic of new neurons really intrigues me and I have written about it before on the blog (www.otherlobe. com) that, as I mentioned earlier, started this book. Some of the blog posts fit nicely with a point made in this book. Where that happens, I have chosen to cite them in a footnote, giving a brief summary and a link to the full blog post. The idea is to flesh out a topic by interweaving a new format without stopping the flow of the text. As a reader, please enjoy them; or if you prefer, skip them entirely.

The first blog post I will cite (Blog Footnote 5.1)[2] is by an undergraduate researcher who worked with a faculty member on the formation of new neurons in the HVC region of the bird's brain. It suggests that the birds may have to do well in the production of the song to have the new neurons survive in the HVC brain area. We can further suppose that a songbird that starts to sings well is highly positively engaged in the task, and we will consider positive emotions in depth in the next chapter, under the topic of neuroeconomics. For now, I would like to suggest the intriguing possibility that brain plasticity may be associated with being positive, engaged, and enthusiastic in learning the task. While

---

2 Blog Footnote 5.1. *Bird Brains: A Model for Expanding the Human Mind in College?* by Shoshana Korman and Jim Stellar, posted on 10/17/2011 (http://otherlobe.com/412/). In this post we discuss how new neurons are born in the brains of song birds, discuss the lab's finding that the song must be well executed for the new neurons to survive. We speculate about whether the pleasure of that accomplishment is involved in the new neuron's survival. Finally, Shoshana wonders as an undergraduate whether she was making new neurons in her brain while she was happily learning new laboratory skills that would advance her own career.

this conclusion is a bit of a stretch from studies of birds' brains, it shows up in other ways, as we will see.

It is a truism among educators that people who are not actively engaged do not learn as well as people who are engaged. Until recently, we may not have suspected that emotional factors may play a role in major brain changes. That phenomenon needs more research, but that possibility clearly exists. And it is going to show up again and again in our analysis of higher education programs.

New Myelination

Aside from adding new neurons, are there other ways that the brain can change its basic structure? The answer is yes. In his book on high performers mentioned above, Daniel Coyle, argues that for individuals to achieve exceptional, or outlier, performance, their practice has to be focused and take place over a long period of time. Coyle visited talent hot spots around the world where award-winning athletes, musicians, and others seem to develop rapidly to a very high level of skill. In analyzing why, he concluded that the first step is to engage the person deeply, something he calls "ignition." As the word suggests, it involves firing up a passion for the activity. Then comes the focused practice, often in a tight community, under coaches, and typically for display to that community later. Sometimes the practice is in one-on-one sessions led by a charismatic coach who inspires everyone to work hard for a goal. The result is that the students not only put in the time, but they do so believing they will emerge as champions. Their practice is "highly mindful," to use a term made famous by Harvard professor Ellen Langer some years ago. In fact, to call these people Coyle met highly mindful seems to do them an injustice. These people often are hyper-mindful about acquiring their skill. The time they put in, which can be years, is much more effective than the time spent in mindless response to satisfy a nagging parent who says, "Practice that piano."

Neuroscientists know that over childhood and adolescence the brain further develops what is called myelination. Myelin is a substance that wraps around the neuron to make it more energy efficient and markedly faster in conducting the communication signal, the axon potential, that neurons send to each other. Coyle argues that the brain can change the myelination of major pathways based on the activity of the neurons driven by practice. If you remember or have heard of the old dial-up Internet service from the early 1990s and compare it to the broadband connections we have today, you can relate to the speed changes that Coyle argues happen when one undertakes years of focused practice. According to that thinking, a skilled violinist can move her fingers faster on the violin, hear more acutely the notes she produces, and maybe can even think faster than we do about the music composition.

We can appreciate the violinist's mastery even if we cannot match it, or even understand how she does it. Even if she were a child prodigy, she did not start out as an outlier. Beyond having an initial skill advantage, she became excellent by dedicated mindful practice, over many years. Was myelination the neural mechanism or at least one of them? More research is required, but a growing group of neuroscientists is studying the effect of neuronal activity on myelin formation. Another undergraduate and I looked into this research and wrote a blog post (Blog Footnote 5.2)[3]. I am now convinced that changes in neuronal myelination could be a factor.

Brain Area Re-mapping: Three Examples

The formation of new neurons and altering the myelin on existing neurons are two ways the brain can change its structure with experience. Brain area re-mapping is another, but this mechanism does not operate at the cellular level. It happens at the level of brain regions.

3 Blog Footnote 5.2. *Magic Myelin* by Lauren Blachorsky and Jim Stellar, posted 3/10/2013 (http://otherlobe.com/magic-myelin/) Myelin may well grow with activity of neurons as Coyle suggested in his book. This blog post examines the potential cellular mechanisms. It supports the idea that this process occurs and sees it as another form of brain change that can underlie the effects of sustained learning in a college education.

As I have noted, brain re-mapping is not a new idea. But viewed through the lens of a dogma that says the adult brain is largely hard-wired, it is natural to suggest that if you lose a visual area due to a stroke, you will be blind just the same as if you lost one or both eyes. The same outcome was thought to be true with motor command areas; if the brain area that controlled the right arm was destroyed by stroke or tumor or some other injury, the person was out of luck, unless he was a young child with a still-developing brain.

In 1998, Michael Merzenich, who is a professor at the University of California, San Francisco, published a famous study on cortical plasticity. In it, he experimented on an adult monkey by interrupting the nerve input from one finger of one hand. As he predicted, when the nerve was interrupted, the neural activity in the brain area that was associated with processing that sensory input from the finger ceased completely. Simple enough. But when the researchers examined the monkey three weeks later, they found something remarkable: The nerve inputs from the two fingers adjacent to the one with the interrupted nerve were starting to take over the previously silent cortical area. The brain was re-mapping itself on the basis of the continuous stimulation coming from the neighboring fingers. If we can be anthropomorphic for a moment, the brain seemed to be saying to itself, "Why let this perfectly good cortical processing potential go to waste? If finger number three does not use it, there is always input from fingers two and four to process."

That kind of re-mapping had been seen before in patients with eye disease. If a person has degeneration of the retina at the spot that provides high-acuity vision, called the fovea, the brain seems to learn to use the areas just around the damaged area. If you converse with such a patient, she often appears to be looking at the top of your head rather than your face, because she is taking aim at your face using the part of the retina that is adjacent to the damaged fovea. If she aimed the fovea directly at your face, she would not see you.

That clinical condition in humans can be replicated in monkeys. In the same way, the silent areas of the visual cortex in the monkey brain, where the visual input can no longer reach, are taken over in time by visual input from the retinal areas around the damaged fovea. Cortical brain regions that once were silent now become active, but with re-wired input from neighboring portions of the retina. Vision researchers have even found some evidence that the acuity of these visual inputs is a bit better than one would expect from the density of the receptors in that part of the retina. It is as though the extra processing from using the once silent brain area is helping to improve visual function.

Does the same thing happen with motor function? Edward Taub, from his animal research, developed for humans what he calls a "constraint-induced movement therapy" for stroke recovery. The method is designed to help people learn to move again by triggering that kind of re-mapping in adults. Suppose, for example, that you had a stroke in the brain area that controlled the right arm, which you now cannot move. Taub's clinicians would put your left arm in a sling to force you to try to use the right arm. You would be assigned a therapist to keep you working at simple exercises designed to get you to make any movement at all with the right arm. As movement of the right arm slowly returns, the exercises would escalate. Eventually you, the patient, would take over, your desire to do the exercises driven by the beginning ability to use the affected arm until recovery becomes substantial.

A key to the method is that the patient must try to move the affected arm to regain function. If she or he merely uses the other arm, the affected arm will never recover. Notice that in Merzenich's monkey study, in which the nerve of the finger was severed, the middle and fourth fingers subsequently were providing tons of input as the monkey kept using its hand. Similar effort was also maintained in the visual example in the areas right around the damaged fovea. And don't forget Coyle's findings on the effort expended by the athletes and musicians who were learning to perform skills at an elite level. If one does not try, hard, brain re-mapping does not work. Getting the re-mapping to work after damage requires therapy that generates lots of input to the brain areas that must change.

Perhaps the most remarkable form of this recovery is what is called "sensory substitution." It is a most extreme version of re-mapping, which Paul Bach-y-Rita, studied for many years at the University of Wisconsin-Madison among other places. At the start of his research, he had blind people (and blindfolded, sighted people) sit in a moveable chair, to which a camera and a computer were attached; in addition, mounted at the back of the chair was a vibrating panel of small squares, against which the subject could lean. When researchers would place shapes and objects in front of the camera, the computer would recreate the image as a series of small vibrations on the chair panel. If the camera was pointed at a triangle, a triangular vibrating pattern was formed against the person's back. With practice, these people began to react to visual objects.

In today's version, the vibrating panel is replaced by a tongue depressor with an electrode array that can produce a pattern of activation through weak electrical stimulation to the tongue; patients say it feels like champagne bubbles. The camera is worn on a headband and the computer rides in a pocket. Again, if the camera looks at a triangle, the tongue depressor makes a triangle pattern of stimulation on the tongue. After much practice using the device to navigate around, people become pretty good at this sensory substitution. In my classes, I would often show a picture of a blind person using the system to climb a climbing wall. The tongue is no retina; it lacks the retina's millions of receptors, and so it generates a lower-quality image. But the people using it are still impressive in what they can do.

Does the same change in neural structure from experience work with cognition? Merzenich, the neuroscientist mentioned previously in connection with the finger denervation experiment, thinks it does.[4] He

4 Michael Merzenich, "Growing Evidence for Brain Plasticity." "On the Elastic Brain." TED talk, February 2004. Accessed January 13, 2015. http://www.ted.com/talks/michael_merzenich_on_the_elastic_brain

has started a company, Posit Science Corp., to apply the theories of brain remapping to conditions ranging from autism to age-related cognitive decline. I will leave it to science and the marketplace to weigh the value of any company or specific piece of research. My point: We are at the dawn of a new era where we know the brain can change, even if we are only beginning to appreciate all the ways it can change. This era will be very exciting for education, especially in developing systems and methods to engage students deeply.

New Synapses, Dendritic Spines, and Hebb's "Fire Together, Wire Together"

Before we leave this discussion of neuroplasticity, let's go back to the neurons from the regional re-mapping discussion above. Donald Hebb, one of the founders of modern neuroscience, famously wrote, "Neurons that fire together, wire together." That principle—that synapses change their connections with other neurons on the basis of activity—seems firmly established today, though the molecular and genetic biochemistry involved remains the subject of intense and fascinating research.

Some research is focused on what happens between the incoming input from one neuron, the axon terminal, and the receiving dendrite from another. On that dendrite is a small protuberance called a dendritic spine. We have mentioned these dendritic spines before, in Chapter 3. Here is where the nervous system is at the smallest scale we have discussed, its most fine-grained and also its most plastic. These spines come and go constantly, some of them moving out to meet the incoming axon input, or moving back and even disappearing entirely.

I find it both ironic and amazing that one of the simple definitions of things that are alive that young children use— things that move on their own—applies to these fine details of our brain structure. Every moment, a brain is the site of all kinds of microscopic movements in the precise way neurons touch one another through these spines. Even by a child's perspective, which associates movement with life, the brain is alive.

The movements of the dendritic spines and other changes in the synaptic connections of neurons are driven by activity. Neurons are active when they are stimulated, either by something from the environment, the body, or another part of the brain. Some neurons seem to be active on their own or are in circuits that loop back on themselves and keep the neural activity going. Thoughts are a reflection of brain activity, and that activity drives other neurons and can establish patterns, like the salivary-control neurons did for Pavlov's dogs, which learned to take their cue from the bell Ivan Pavlov rang. As every school kid knows, Pavlov's dogs salivated when he rang the bell. But that only happened after those dogs had experience that paired the ringing of the bell with meat powder placed in their mouths. The automatic response was acquired, we now know, because the brain rewired itself, just as Hebb said. The difference today is that with modern methods to visualize these tiny pieces of brain cells under a high-powered microscope, we can actually see it.

The Hebbian plasticity of the brain has been known and taught in all the textbooks since I was a college student. We also have known for a while that certain brain areas, such as the hippocampus, seem to help us store the daily facts and theories that we learn and could declare if asked. As part of that hippocampal research, we also learned long ago that other kinds of learning of a more background or procedural nature exist, such as speaking our native language or performing a well-learned routine like driving a car.

We knew that sensory systems changed with experience. I remember being taught in graduate school about how the isolated leg ganglion of a cockroach could learn to lift that leg out of a bath if an electric shock was triggered when the leg touched the bath. I remember thinking then that if the isolated leg ganglion of a cockroach could learn, then every part of a human nervous system should be able learn, whether it was tasked with learning facts or simple automatic habits and reflexes.

The notion that neurons fired together are wired together was enough for me and I happily went off to a 35-year career in academics, teaching for at least 20 of them that Hebbian synapse was the way we learned. I had no idea that, by not questioning whether the adult brain was hard wired, I was propagating an over-broad generalization. But science is like that. We think we have a firm understanding, until someone comes along and shows that our understanding is, at best, partial. Newton's theory gets incorporated into and replaced by Einstein's theory. Hard-wired brains give way to brains that can change.

Even if that change requires a great deal of time and effort and even if, I, the neuroscientist, must wait patiently for more research, I, the educator, want to take lessons that I can use right away to make my institution better at educating its students. To me, that lesson is one of optimism about how much we can help our students learn and grow if we can find the right triggers of their own inspiration.

CHAPTER 6:

Unconscious Emotional Decision Making

It's a universal experience: You are occupied with one activity, like driving, and an idea about something you'd been thinking of earlier in the day pops into your head. A solution to a problem, for example—perhaps a really tough one that earlier had seemed unsolvable. Somehow, the solution was unavailable, until now, when it just appears. Or, here's another common experience: You are trying to remember a friend's name in conversation, being utterly unable to grasp it from memory; but suddenly, in the middle of another activity, it comes to you.

What is happening here? It may seem as if you have two brains working in your head—a first brain, of which you are aware and which you command, and a second brain, which works outside of your awareness and control, presenting you with ideas, conclusions, and solutions, or taking on entire problems solo. It seems that way, because it is. Let's go a little deeper.

We all know we have unconscious systems to take care of motor activities. No one is surprised that you can sit straight, keep your head up, or walk without falling while concentrating on something else. What surprises most people is that unconscious processes govern or powerfully influence other types of decisions, such as forming and expressing biases and making key life choices—even in choosing a college major, career, or life partner.

We do have words for this operation. I originally called the blog *The Other Lobe of the Brain* to get at the idea. In this book I use the more technical term "limbic system" or refer to the mammalian brain as the location where such processes may occur. A classical anatomical reference was made by an artist who has blogged with me and used the term "heart reasons" to refer to this kind of mental process (Blog Footnote 6.1)[1]. Whatever the terminology I use, I never have difficulty convincing artists that part of their brain is beyond their awareness. Artists accept that; they often just say that the unconscious brain is where their creativity originates.

In this chapter, which builds on the previous one on neuroplasticity, I make the claim that underlies the rest of this book: that learning from experience naturally taps into unconscious brain mechanisms with particular alacrity, and that the learning that happens there changes you—how your brain makes judgments, develops skills, applies knowledge, works in teams, and even thinks in ways of which you are unaware.

I also use this point to argue that experience-based learning could give colleges an opportunity to combine learning from those unconscious brain circuits with more conscious learning in the classroom. By combining

---

1 Blog Footnote 6.1. *Heart/Mind, Art*, by Antonella Mason and Jim Stellar, posted 2/25/212 (http://otherlobe.com/469/). AM is an artist who includes heart-mind issues in her art. We had many discussions about art and neuroscience that are reflected in this blog. Early on in the blog this sentence appears, "JS says that he almost always find that artists think in an 'other lobe' fashion, perhaps because creativity is something of a mystery to the cognitive mind (Where did that idea come from?), yet this is where artists live."

them, we produce a more mature student who is better at leveraging classroom knowledge and who is more employment ready.

As I have previously suggested, we can thank the fMRI machine for our modern understanding of the unconscious brain circuits that help us make decisions beyond our awareness. But I need to add a caveat. Back when I was an assistant professor of psychology at Harvard, I heard a talk by the neuroanatomist Walle Nauta, who pronounced, "The presumption of originality in scholarship is usually the result of poor library work." His words come back to me whenever I am about to award exclusive credit to research based on the fMRI machine. The role of unconscious processes in human behavior, thinking, and learning has long been recognized, perhaps most famously by Freud and his followers, but also by many others in psychology, philosophy, and education.

With homage to all who have gone before, then, let us proceed into this world of decisions that are largely hidden from our awareness.

Neuroeconomics: Weighing Risk and Reward

You've seen cartoons showing an angel and a devil, one standing on each shoulder of someone making a decision — say, to buy an expensive leather jacket. "You would look marvelous in that jacket," the devil says. The prospect of owning it brightens your day and makes you feel good. The angel reminds you, however, that the money should really be used to pay your credit card bill or to save for your child's college tuition.

Buy it, or not? Facing the decision makes you a little queasy in the stomach. Yes, your gut is involved. Deep in your brain, at least two limbic-related brain structures, the nucleus accumbens and the insular cortex, are fighting it out, on an unconscious level, even as you consciously balance reward and risk.

I experienced that very conflict, complete with the queasy stomach, on a family vacation in Florence, Italy. My wife and older daughter were at a museum, and I was killing time in the market with my younger daughter, when we happened into a leather shop. And there it was: the leather jacket of my dreams. It was expensive, and there was only one in my size.

Unable to confer with my wife, I hemmed and hawed. My child wondered what was wrong with me. Why couldn't I just make a decision? After all, there was gelato to be eaten just down the street. But at that moment, I was not in charge of my emotions. I had to wait until my internal conflict subsided, or at least tipped toward one side or the other. It took a few minutes, but I did buy the jacket. Every time I put it on, I break into a little dance, at least in my mind.

The field of neuroeconomics seeks to understand that kind of monetary decision process in the brain. Using the fMRI as an experimental tool, scientists may observe the brain of someone making a decision about a purchase or using information to balance reward and risk in other ways. Money decisions are good to study; the behavioral result can be quantified. And everybody is interested in money — researchers, their subjects, universities, and other institutions. In the wake of the financial crisis and recession of the early 2000s, a lot of attention is being paid to understanding how people think about money and investments. That interest has made neuroeconomics a hot growth industry in academia, along with behavioral economics and some related fields.[2]

The Precise Mathematics of the Unconscious Brain

Before going further into neuroeconomics, I want to establish an important notion: Behavior is highly quantitative—and, here, I am not talking about money. You may think you are bad in math, and you may

---

2 The term "neuroeconomics" is of recent vintage, brought into wide use by *Neuroeconomics: Decision Making and the Brain,* edited by Glimcher, Camera, Fehr, Poldrack. 2008. Many people credit the coinage to the senior editor, Professor Paul Glimcher, for use of the term in his earlier papers.

consciously avoid mathematical tasks, but your brain does not. It is built to process information and often does so with great precision. For example, many people are pretty good at predicting the trajectory of a hit baseball, so they know where to move their body to place a gloved hand precisely in the path of the ball to make the catch. That's the unconscious brain using math for motor behavior. Could it also do the math for other types of decisions, such as choosing between alternatives?

Our formal understanding of such calculations at a behavioral level begins with B. F. Skinner, as mentioned previously. We honor him as a psychologist every time we use the words "reinforcement" or "operant behavior." Skinner liked data. He especially liked orderly data that, when plotted on a graph, would create a smooth curve, relating a behavioral property, such as rate at which a hungry rat presses a lever, to a controlling variable, such as the size or frequency of the food reinforcement for doing so. Rats, pigeons, humans—they all delivered what Skinner wanted, creating a degree of order in the study of "operant behavior" that made it, for a time, the talk of the field of psychology.

When I was a young assistant professor in Harvard's psychology department, Skinner was an emeritus professor, near the end of his career. I would occasionally sit with Fred, as we called him, for lunch in what was then the William James Hall cafeteria I would show him my research data, from which I was trying to relate a rat's pressing of a lever to brain mechanisms that were activated by rewarding direct electrical stimulation of a particular deep brain structure.

I had heard stories that Skinner disliked neuroscientists, because those of my ilk were attempting to decipher brain function before the behavioral psychologists had figured out operant psychology. It was said that he thought we were acting like mechanics evaluating a car for the first time by looking under its hood before we figured out how to drive it. Yet Fred, I found, was charming as well as brilliant and not the least bit hostile to my work or field. Of course, I was also flattered by receiving attention from a legendary pioneer of operant behavior.

As I also mentioned previously, that operant behavior research had been taken to the next level of quantitation by Richard Herrnstein, a former student of Skinner's, who was also a professor at Harvard while I was there. Along with others, Herrnstein showed the mathematical precision of the matching law, a principle of how animals and humans make decisions about allocating their time and energy when choice was involved. In their studies, a hungry rat is placed in an operant chamber with two levers to press to get food. It can only press one lever at a time. When the levers were set so that one lever released twice as much food as the other lever, the studies found, the rat would spend twice as much time pressing it. If the experimenter adjusted the mechanism so that one lever produced three times as much reinforcement or reward as the other lever, the rat figured that out and pressed the lever three times as often. Humans do the same thing.

Behavior of both humans and rats also reveals a trade-off between the amount of reward and delay of that reward. Most people feel that delaying a reward, even a little bit, weakens its impact. Anyone who has trained a dog knows that a treat needs to be given to the dog right after it completes the task, if the treat is to be effective in controlling behavior. Delay weakens the impact of the reward.

On university campuses, students, like most of us, will generally opt for immediate gratification, even if it puts at risk a longer-term reward. That late-night party often outweighs studying to get a better chance of excelling on an exam the next morning. Most of us stay at the party a little too long, rather than study or sleep to be sharp for the test. And some of us buy the leather jacket even when worried about the expense.

The Nucleus Accumbens and the Insular Cortex

The angel and the devil, as you might have guessed, correspond with structures in the brain. The nucleus accumbens is the devil expressing the psychological force of reward; and the insular cortex is the angel presenting the psychological force of risk. The balance between those two forces is the basis for neuroeconomics.

In the almost 40 years that I spent studying the nucleus accumbens of the brains of rats, my research goal was a better understanding of the neuroscience of human reward processes. My real-world goal was to help loosen the terrible grip that drugs like cocaine have on the brains and lives of addicted people. In both humans and rats, the accumbens, sitting in the middle of the brain, receives a squirt of the neurotransmitter dopamine from a small nucleus located just behind it called the ventral tegmental area.

Neuroscientists generally accept, based on animal research, that dopamine in the nucleus accumbens is involved in feeling reward. As we have discussed, drugs such as amphetamine and cocaine produce euphoria by boosting dopamine in the accumbens, beginning the cycle of addiction. So it is no surprise that, when people make money, fMRI scans show that dopamine is present, activating the accumbens.

The insular cortex—cast as our long-suffering angel—is, as its name implies, buried deep in the cortex, which makes it seem to be insulated from the brain's surface. This area does many things, one of which, we think, may be to help track the risk associated with various behaviors, like buying something that is expensive. We wrote about the insular cortex, risk, and unconscious decision-making (Blog Footnote 6.2)[3].

Several fMRI studies have looked at the interplay between activity in the accumbens and the insular cortex. Subjects have played games that

---

3 Blog Footnote 6.2 *Making Emotional Choices; It May Be the Only Way We Know How*, by Raphael Spiro & Golshan Aghanori (posted 1/26/13), http://otherlobe.com/making-emotional-choices-it-may-be-the-only-way-we-know-how/ - Three of us set out to explain the insula cortex in lay terms. We all shared a general education course I taught and where the insula cortex came up in neuroeconomics and in other places, including changes in nicotine craving after a stroke in that location. The idea is that these are all gut decisions

combined risk and reward in making economic decisions, while their brains were being scanned. A 2006 review[4] examined one of these neuroeconomics psychology experiments, called the Iowa Gambling Task. In this experiment, subjects are asked to draw cards from one of a small number of decks, typically four. Each deck contains cards that give the subject money and cards that take money away. The decks are different and some are more favorable than others. Subjects are not told which deck is which. They have to figure it out from experience, trying the cards in the decks and seeing what happens. After a while, people are choosing from the deck that is most favorable. Of course, inside the brain, the areas that track risk and reward are showing corresponding activity on the fMRI.

A surprising aspect of this study is how closely the activity in these brain areas was related to the subjects' bodily states and their decisions. For example, in one study, a researcher measured tiny changes in the electrical conductivity of the subjects' skin as it sweats under stress. That measure, called the galvanic skin-conductance response, is also used in the lie detector test. The data was collected while the subjects were in the early phases of learning the Iowa Gambling Task and had not yet figured out the decks. Fascinatingly, when they were poised to choose the most dangerous deck, which held cards that took away money more often than they awarded it, their galvanic skin-conductance response went up, indicating stress, well before they had consciously developed a strategy of which deck to choose. The emotional systems that made the body sweat had figured out the nature of the decks before the conscious mind did (Blog Footnote 6.3)[5]. These decisions and strategies can get quite complicated in social situations when we interact with others in such neuroeconomic decisions, particularly

---

4 A nice summary of the research in "The Role of Emotion in Decision Making: A Cognitive Neuroscience Perspective" by Nasir Naqvi, Baba Shiv, and Antoine Bechara, published in the journal *Current Directions in Psychological Science* in 2006. That work comes in part from an important center, Brain and Creativity Institute, and Department of Psychology, University of Southern California, established by Antonio Damasio.

5 Blog Footnote 6.3 *Social Neuroeconomics – Over bidding*, by Raphael Spiro and Jim Stellar, Posted 1/27/12 (http://otherlobe.com/social-neuroeconomics---over-bidding/). It has been known for a long time that social conditions influence a person's decisions. Here is where the common term "social pressure" has its origins. In these studies, social conditions are applied to neuroeconomics experiments where some surprising brain areas are activated (or deactivated) when people compete, lose, and overbid the next time. Different brain areas seem to be involved when people followed the head in their buying behavior.

when strategy is involved about how the others might play the game (Blog Footnote 6.4)[6].

We will return to this phenomenon when we discuss how the unconscious brain circuits that estimate what is good for us may communicate with our conscious minds through emotions, without conscious mathematical analysis. "The heart has reasons of which reason does not know," wrote mathematician and philosopher Blaise Pascal[7] in one of my favorite quotations. In my view and in this book, the unconscious brain circuits are the heart. The question for educators is: Can we design and deliver a college experience that engages the "hearts" of our students?

I don't want to leave you with the simplistic idea that only two brain areas are involved in decisions about risk and reward. Other areas are clearly involved. One clue is that the galvanic skin-conductance response does not occur in patients with damage to the ventral medial prefrontal cortex. That brain area seems to keep track of past emotional reactions to your choices, such as, in the Iowa Gambling Task, the major disappointment subjects feel when they hit a big money-taking card in one of the decks. That brain area seems to re-create that emotion when subjects contemplate making the same choice again. "Once bitten, twice shy," as the old saying goes. People with brain damage in that spot would not be so shy about trying again despite having been disappointed previously.

Interestingly, it is this anticipation of an emotional consequence to a choice that may contribute to our making the proper trade-off between alternatives, such as delay and amount, as mentioned earlier. In my experience as an educator, sooner or later, most students learn the consequences of prioritizing partying over exams; they repeat that mistake less often. We call that maturity. We cannot say definitively that the ventral medial prefrontal

---

6 Blog Footnote 6.4 *Neurobargining – Ex Ed brain circuits in action?*, by Alexandra Hilbert and Jim Stellar, Posted on 2/12/12 (http://otherlobe.com/neurobargining—-ex-ed-brain-circuits-in-action/). Modern cognitive neurology can get pretty bizarre, even in a field like economics. Consider this blog post where people are trying to "psych each other out" in figuring out strategies to take advantage of the other. There is a brain area for that, or so it appears and who knows how this is relevant to trying to choose a major in college.

7 *Le cœur a ses raisons, que la raison ne connaît point.*

cortex area of the brain, working with the accumbens and insular cortex, mediates this maturity, but something likely changes in these brain circuits that might be worth further investigation.

Before we go further, let's consider for a moment another system, the visual system, that illustrates well how unconscious processes work to shape our conscious behavior. Like all mammals, humans have an old visual system that functions along with our newer conscious vision system. For example, we generally put our eyes on a person, place, or thing that has our attention. Likewise, when we look at an object, it is typically what our attention is focused on. But there can be startling disconnects, especially with brain damage.

In the 1980s, an experimental psychologist at Oxford University, Lawrence Weiskrantz, discovered a patient with damage to his primary visual area who reported being blind in the corresponding visual field. Yet somehow the patient could guess verbally the simple geometric shapes that were flashed into what he perceived as the blind part of his visual field. How could he speak about what he could not see? In 1990, Weiskrantz wrote a book, *BlindSight*, about his remarkable disconnection of function and I refer you to it and his work. Remember that I have mentioned another book, Oliver Sacks' *The Man Who Mistook His Wife for a Hat*. This phenomenon, in which connections that normal people detect seem disconnected in brain damaged patients, is not limited to vision. In that case, it seems reasonable that unconscious brain circuits could function independently of the conscious functioning of which we are aware.

Going back to neuroeconomics, many more brain areas are involved in circuits of interest. For example, the posterior inferior frontal cortex seems to tell the brain when it has enough information to make a decision. The amygdala region of the brain, which was once thought to be involved primarily in fear conditioning, appears to have other, broader roles in emotional behavior; its versatility is not entirely surprising given its multifaceted structure and rich connections to other brain areas. But in our neuroeconomics analysis of risk versus reward, we need to understand only two points for now. First, these various areas may be part of an elaborate, powerful circuit that helps a person balance choices largely using emotional brain systems to anticipate the consequences. Second, this circuit appears to add a stream of input from feelings or emotion to the person's rational, calculated, and conscious decision-making process.

Long before the fMRI machine, psychologists Daniel Kahneman and Amos Tversky had begun to discover that humans use shortcuts to make decisions, using processes that are often unconscious and often very rapid. As mentioned before, in 2002, Kahneman shared the Nobel Prize in Economics for "for having integrated insights from psychological research into economic science, especially concerning human judgment and decision-making under uncertainty."[8] His partner, Tversky, had died by then and could not share in the honor, which is not awarded posthumously.

If you think these ideas are limited only to psychology or economics research and do not have influence on our lives, look back to 1996, when Alan Greenspan, then the chairman of the Federal Reserve, coined the phrase "irrational exuberance" to characterize a stock market that he felt was rising in an unsustainable manner. Robert J. Shiller, a Nobel Prize-winning economist at Yale turned that idea into two books that predicted the rupturing of economic bubbles—the first being the dot-com bubble and the second the more recent sub-prime mortgage bubble.

Most of us do not recognize that we are in an economic bubble until it bursts. Maybe if we knew enough about how the neuroeconomics-related areas of our brains worked, we could predict when we were all headed into a bubble.

How could we apply neuroeconomics to higher education? There is, of course, the cost of higher education. Some students are weighing

8 In 2011, in the fMRI era, Daniel Khaneman elaborated on his findings in *Thinking, Slow and Fast*.

the risks and opportunities of attending college against those of working. "Time is money," as Benjamin Franklin said. But within college, the time allocation by the student to study one field over another is a neuroeconomics decision, as much as buying a one object over another. We just tend not to think of it that way in higher education, at least not yet.

The Origin of Good and Bad Feelings in Old Parts of the Brain

The good and bad feelings that seem to be involved in decision making—and are thus a focus of our neuroeconomics discussion—are part of even more basic brain processes. They came from structures of the brain, like the hypothalamus, that developed earliest in human evolution. And they are part of the basic homeostatic regulation of the body that is necessary for life itself.

Homeostasis is the process that keeps our blood and extracellular fluid within a narrow range of a proper chemical composition. This is important, as the environment would immediately kill most of our body cells if they were exposed to it directly. Our cells need to be immersed in a solution similar to seawater, which is the purpose of our blood. The brain helps us to ingest just the right balance of water and salt to keep the blood properly composed. Being short of water gives rise to a powerful thirst; if we don't slake it we begin to feel ill. It is very unpleasant to be very thirsty. Consuming water to satisfy that thirst, on the other hand, is very pleasurable.

Many ideas were connected to this homeostasis and hypothalamic history that did not have to do directly with feeding or drinking behavior. For example, Olds and Milner discovered as early as 1954[9] that electrical stimulation of the brain was rewarding. They demonstrated that fact by getting rats to press a lever to turn on the stimulation. Even earlier,

9 Olds, J. and Milner, P. Positive reinforcement produced by electrical stimulation of septal area and other regions of rat brain. *Journal of Computational Physiology and Psychology.* 1954, 47(6):419-27.

Walter Hess showed something similar as part of his 1949 Nobel Prize-winning work on brain stimulation of the mid-portions of the brain that sometimes produced a purring reactions in cats. Not to compare myself to these giants, but I did my own PhD thesis on the related topic of the hypothalamus and approaching and withdrawing behaviors in rats in the late 1970s, as mentioned, in the laboratory of professor Randy Gallistel. I showed in my thesis that rewarding stimulation of the lateral hypothalamus activates a pattern of reflexes of approach to external stimuli and at the same time a pattern of decreases in reflexes of withdrawal. Stimulation to the neighboring medial hypothalamus, which the rats did not like, produced the opposite pattern of decreasing approach and increasing withdrawal reflexes. I got the same result when I compromised the function of the lateral hypothalamus by destroying a bit of its tissue with a small brain lesion. Remember, the lateral and medial hypothalamus function like a seesaw; pushing down on one side makes the other side go up. These subjects with lateral hypothalamic lesions were biased toward withdrawal in their reflexes and in their operant behavior. Thus, I saw in the hypothalamus the positive and negative influences at a low level of function in the brain of which Antonio Damasio [10] later wrote in his book about consciousness at a high level.

What have we learned to this point? We know that within each of us and certainly all mammals are primordial unconscious processes that try to keep us physiologically healthy by directing our behavior, indeed our feelings, toward things we need to survive. Those things start with homeostasis, then nourishment, and avoiding toxic substances or dangerous situations that cause illness or injury. The primordial feelings are part of circuits that include the accumbens and the insular cortex.

At that point in the nervous system, pleasure and pain may become opportunity and risk. They become the neuroeconomics decisions of the purchase of a stock or the commitment to a major in college. Importantly,

---

10 Damiaso, Antonio. *Self Comes to Mind: Constructing the Conscious Brain*, Vintage Books, New York, NY 2012.

we tend not to be fully aware of these processes. We tend not to know when we use a simpler heuristic to solve a more complex problem. We just know it is fun, or not fun. And perhaps, in our enthusiasm, we buy too much stock or hold onto it too long because we are averse to taking the loss of selling it at a lower price than we wanted. Daniel Kahneman and his colleagues thought so.

To take it a step further, these body-sense feelings and emotions are thought by some to be a necessary part of how our conscious minds work. While further pursuit of this topic in this chapter takes us too far afield, much has been studied and written about it by Damasio, the director of the Brain and Creativity Institute at the University of Southern California.[11] I find his 2010 book title, *Self Comes to Mind: Constructing the Conscious Brain*, to be very revealing. I also find fascinating his concept of self that has its origins in this body wellness sense beginning with homeostasis.

Gut Feelings

Ever get the feeling that something is not quite right? In the introduction to *Blink*, Malcolm Gladwell writes about an art expert who saw a Classical statue at the J. Paul Getty museum in California and an immediate feeling that it was a fraud. The museum had made a lengthy study of the work's provenance, composition, and style before buying the piece. How did the expert know it was a fake? And why did the museum not know?

The art expert was very experienced. He had spent a great deal of time at his craft. According to Gladwell, he had trained his entire brain, both the conscious and unconscious parts. The conscious training included remembering facts and figures and being able to talk about art. But he had also trained his eye, in ways of which he was likely unaware. That expert eye was part of his unconscious decision-making system; it had become very

---

11 http://dornsife.usc.edu/bci/

good at detecting when something was out of order or did not fit. That's the part that raised the red flag the moment he saw the artwork.

Let me explain how this works with reward detection. I have mentioned already that we believe the dopamine neurons of the ventral tegmental area project to the nucleus accumbens help to produce the experience of reward. The question then becomes what excites those dopamine neurons. Neuroscientists know that those dopamine neurons get inputs from a variety of brain areas from below the ventral tegmental area in the lower brain stem and from above in the higher brain including even excitatory connections from the frontal cortex. Let's suppose that when the brain detects a homeostatic correction (e.g. water when we are thirsty) it fires the dopamine neurons. That establishes the basic reward effect. Let's further suppose that the higher areas of the brain keep track of which stimuli are associated with that water source, giving us a brain mechanism for making the nervous system anticipate what leads to the water we want and to any other rewarding stimulus.

What is not so obvious is that sitting right there in the ventral tegmental area and as neighbors to the dopamine neurons are neurons that use a different neurotransmitter called most often by its abbreviated name of GABA, though its long name is gamma-aminobutyric acid. GABA is neurotransmitter that inhibits other neurons, including the dopamine neurons. So, who controls the GABA neurons? In part, other higher brain areas do. The resulting effect is simple and was famously discovered and pursued by Wolfram Schultz starting about 20 years ago. Here is the basic finding: When an animal is presented initially with an attractive stimulus, and chocolate would do it for me, the dopamine neurons fire. We think they may encode the euphoric or pleasurable effects of the stimulus and perhaps importantly generate motivational effects as well to get the human or animal going to get the reward. If the reward stimulus is repeated and becomes predicted by a cue, then the dopamine starts firing to the cue and, interestingly, it fires less to the actual primary stimulus, the chocolate in this case. Then, if something predicts that cue, the dopamine release will move to that stimulus. This operation leads to a chain of reward-predictive events that are now occurring in the brain, producing dopamine release to the cue but also suppressing it to the original stimulus.

What does this chain of stimulus control have to do with our story? Well if something changes in the environment and the reward comes earlier in the chain or is bigger than expected, the dopamine release to the reward is larger than expected. If the reward is missing or comes later than expected, then the learned suppressive influences are not balanced by the activation of the dopamine neurons in response to the reward stimulus, and the dopamine neurons can go silent, or at least well below their baseline activity. This is the reward-prediction effect.

We can flip the reward though, and look at stimuli that create fear or anxiety instead of pleasure. Recent neuroscience research using optical-genetic stimulating or inhibiting techniques on specific neuron circuits within the amygdala circuits of rats seem to show the same thing but with fear conditioning. They could also be in the brainstem or hypothalamus, as we discussed briefly as being associated with fear or anxiety or even pain. The point for me is that every sequence learning possibility that exists in control over the positive reward system also exists in control over the negative emotion-producing system. We are back to the dual primordial feelings, except we have now made them keen, anticipatory, learning systems that use the higher smarter functions of the brain to automatically regulate their activity. And none of this prediction requires our conscious awareness.

How do those feelings get out and into our conscious minds so we can talk about them? We do not know, but here is an idea. There are some very interesting neurons recently discovered in a brain region called the anterior cingulate cortex and reported in a paper by Allman and others in 2006.[12] These neurons are not found in animals below the level

---

12 Seeley WW , Carlin DA, Allman JM, Macedo MN, Bush C, Miller BL, Dearmond SJ Early frontotemporal dementia targets neurons unique to apes and humans. *Annals of Neurology*, 2006, 60(6):660-667

of the primate (except whales) and are most developed in humans. They may receive dopamine and could track the reward prediction error those dopamine neurons generate. The neurons are called von Economo neurons, after their discoverer, Constantin von Economo, who reached the peak of his career in the early 1900s. This topic is so important that we will return to it in Chapter 12. A number of authors have called these neurons to our attention. Damasio does so in *Self Comes to Mind*, when he refers to convergence-divergence zones the neurons seem to connect disparate brain. Again, I will defer to Damasio and others a proper discussion of consciousness.

I also have to say that this chain of neurons going from reward-prediction error in the ventral tegmental area where dopamine neurons originate to the generation of feelings that can and do guide our decision making is not really new. Remember Pavlov's dogs? They salivated to the bell because Pavlov paired it with meat powder presented right after ringing the bell.

Many other people have looked at such sequences of events, even postulating that any stimulus-generated emotion will trigger its opposite when the stimulus departs. In one theory by Solomon and Corbit in their famous 1974 paper,[13] that is the explanation for the craving that suddenly appears right after finishing a satisfying salted potato chip, and it compels one to have another. More seriously, they apply this thinking to drug addiction, where the after-effect grows with repetition from craving to withdrawal agony, and even to the grief reaction when someone's spouse dies particularly after many years of a happy marriage.

We already know that these processes exist within us. This is why the art dealer in *Blink* felt something was wrong. It is why in the Iowa Gambling Task, the stress response appeared as the subject's hand hovered over the deck of cards that contained a high number of money-taking

13 Solomon, R. and Corbit, J. An opponent-process theory of motivation. I. Temporal dynamics of affect. *Psychol. Rev.* 1964, 81:119-45.

versus money-giving cards, and did so before the subject was consciously aware of the nature of the decks. It is why people sometimes tell you to listen to that small voice inside you, go with your gut, or other such phrases that suggest your feelings about something might be relevant to the decision and should not be ignored. You have a great deal of learning that happens in your nervous system and controls the systems that generate these feelings. Much of this learning is likely to be unavailable to the conscious, speaking, thinking you. But it is in there anyway, and it is often trying to tell you something like: that art is not authentic; that guy creeps me out; that major in college or career path is not for me, even if my mother told me that is what I should do with my life.

Beyond Risk to Empathy

We can go beyond the role of the insular cortex's role in risk detection to go to a broader area of involvement that actually involves empathy. To get there we have to first use the psychology term *theory of mind*. This simple concept means that we humans behave toward other humans as though they have a mind. We mentally take their place. We read emotions on the faces of others with ease, and that reading is important in forming the community that is so much a part of the workplace or the classroom or the family—any place that we humans gather. Indeed there has been a whole line of research recently on what are called mirror neurons, first discovered in monkeys in the motor control areas in the late 1990s at the University of Parma in Italy. These neurons, which were involved with motor execution, such as hand-to-mouth feeding movements, fired when the monkey simply saw someone else do the same task. Mirror neurons exist in us and were more recently made famous in a TED Talk by Vilayanur Ramachandran[14] who called them Gandhi neurons, and suggested a special role for them in producing connectedness between humans, allowing us to shift from

---

14 https://www.ted.com/talks/vs_ramachandran_the_neurons_that_shaped_civilization

imitation to empathy. Of course, many laboratories study these neurons and, although some controversy exists, the general consensus seems to be that this brain circuit is important to human interaction. It may even be important to our interaction with animals, which, for example, can be seen when humans and horses get to know each other and seem to agree to work together (Blog Footnote 6.5)[15].

There is much more to discuss on these topics and some of them will come up again in later chapters. For now, let's stick with the insular cortex, or *insula*, as it is often called. Many recent studies have looked at the role of the insula in empathy, a complete topic in itself. One study shows that this brain area is activated when people are merely shown pictures of bodily injury to hands or feet.[16]

It is as though risk, whether of injury or of a purchase decision, and the resulting negative emotion, can be projected cognitively onto another person who is suffering. We have brain circuits that feel their pain in an identification sense, even if we do not feel it literally.

If you think that empathetic ability does not matter, think again. One of the most fascinating tasks in neuroeconomics is the Ultimatum Game, invented in the 1980s. The Ultimatum Game offers insight into why humans often depart from purely rational behavior, even in economic decisions and even though we remain predictable. The game is simple. Here is how it works: You are given some money, say twenty dollars in one-dollar bills. You have to give some of the money to another person, who then gets to decide whether you both keep the money or neither of you gets anything. How much would you give that other person? Rational choice theory from economics says that you would give as little as possible, maybe one dollar. After all, the other person is getting something for nothing, so why should she or he not be satisfied with whatever you give and decide that you both

---

15 Blog Footnote 6.5. *Riding high on horse-human communication*, by Susan Salk and Jim Stellar, posted on 2/21/10 (http://otherlobe.com/riding-high-on-horse-human-communication/) If the human and the horse can communicate as is well known by the term "meeting up" in the horse world, then people can communicate without words and reach joint decisions on how to work together. This blog discusses that form of interspecies non-verbal communication and applies it to experiential education.
16 http://www.jneurosci.org/content/30/10/3739.short

will keep the money? The game is played only once, so there is no chance for hard feelings to build up.

What would you do? Across many cultures, people typically give between a quarter and a half of the money to the other person. It is as though they put themselves in the other person's place, realize that it would be insulting to get one dollar, and allocate an amount that will be accepted. One group of subjects that research show tends not to behave in this way, and instead tends to gives as little as possible following the rational choice theory of economics, is a group whose members often have difficulty recognizing others' point of view: autistic individuals.

A recent study[17] found that people who practice meditation (in this case, in the Buddhist tradition) tend to accept less money in the Ultimatum Game than other groups. The more experience they have in meditation, the less money they find acceptable; in addition, when scanned by a fMRI machine, the insular cortexes of these people's brains are correspondingly less activated. Finally, another even more recent study shows a correlation between people who have a lifetime practice of meditation and also have a larger than average insular cortex.[18]

So do we have an empathy circuit in the brain? I would say yes, although that possibility deserves much more research and it may be important to distinguish between physical pain and social pain that triggers an empathy reaction. A great deal of popular literature has surfaced around research on oxytocin, a natural hormone made in the pituitary of the brain. People claim that oxytocin is the "cuddle drug," as welcome hugs seem to release it in humans and make people more generous in neuroeconomic games like the above-discussed ultimatum game. Administering oxytocin to a person does seem to increase his or her feelings of empathy, as long as the empathy is directed toward someone whom the person considers to be part

17 http://www.frontiersin.org/decision_neuroscience/10.3389/fnins.2011.00049/abstract/. The authors do not speculate which comes first, insula cortex activation or less concern with being cheated. We do not know if empathy or ability to take others into consideration is even involved. Such is the nature of studies that are correlations where two variables are linked but one cannot say which one caused the other or if both were caused by a third factor.
18 http://www.frontiersin.org/Human_Neuroscience/10.3389/fnhum.2012.00034/abstract/

of a favored group. We will return to oxytocin in later chapters. Again, we will return to these topics later in this book.

Altruism

In this chapter so far, we have developed the idea that we have decision circuits in the brain that originate with base feelings of well-being, or its opposite. Without being conscious of them, we relate those primordial feelings to choices about money or investments of our time and energy. So those feelings end up influencing our conscious selves in our daily lives, and possibly figure in high-level processes such as the empathy we feel for another person or animal.

An example of this influence can be seen when the reward process in the nucleus accumbens resists decisions you make consciously for another high-level reason: altruism. To illustrate, consider the true story of a town in Sweden that the Swedish federal government asked to accept a nuclear waste dump as a matter of national need.[19] The town agreed to do so by a 51 percent majority vote. Then the federal government thought better of the plan and decided that it needed to compensate the town's citizens with money. It asked the town to vote again, now with the additional financial incentive. This vote, however, was negative, with only 25 percent in favor.

How could that be? How could adding an incentive actually undermine the town's yes vote? To me, that outcome suggests that a different calculator in the brain was at work during the second vote. The second one made decisions based on a something other than doing what is right, or altruism. It may have decided on the balance between reward and risk, once money was involved.

Another story in which a monetary reward seemed to undermine a positive function starts with a famous old test on creative thinking,

---

19 I first heard this story in Jonah Lehrer's 2012 book *Imagine: How Creativity Works*, but an account of it is also in a later book by Michael Sandel, *What Money Can't Buy: The Moral Limits of Markets (2013)*.

developed by Karl Duncker in Germany and published in 1945. In this test, individuals were given a candle, a book of matches, and a box of thumbtacks. They were asked to use these supplies to attach the candle to the corkboard wall and light it so that the wax would not drip on the floor (i.e., the candle would be upright). Most of us start out by dribbling some hot wax on the wall and trying to attach the candle directly. When that fails, people try to use the tacks to secure the wax to the wall to hold the weight of the candle. As you can guess, none of these strategies work. The only way to succeed is to see the box that holds the thumbtacks as part of the solution and not just a box that holds thumbtacks. The solution is to dump out the tacks, use them to attach the box to the wall, secure the candle in the box (a little hot wax will do that), and light the candle. It typically takes some time to figure that out, to literally think out of the box.

An application to the present discussion comes in a later version of this test published in 1962. In that study, Samuel Glucksberg added a condition. He told some of the subjects that they could win money if they completed the task quickly. But subjects with the financial incentive were actually slower than subjects who had no such incentive. The former took more time to complete the task when they were paid to do it fast than if they had been left to follow their own motivations.

What is going on here? One possibility is that the dopamine released by the nucleus accumbens, and possibly neighboring brain regions, narrows the scope of task-based thinking. It produces focus. In an extreme form, that focusing effect is seen in people addicted to amphetamine (Blog Footnote 6.6)[20], which releases dopamine in the brain. There are stories of speed freaks of the 1960s in San Francisco who would disassemble and assemble the carburetors on their cars seven to eight times in a day.

20 Blog footnote 6.6. *Positive emotional states lead to engagement, focused practice, and mastery*, by Lauren Blachorsky and Jim Stellar, posted on 6/9/13 (http://otherlobe.com/positive-emotional-states-lead-to-engagement-focused-practice-and-mastery/). Dopamine is a neurotransmitter released in the accumbens and elsewhere in the brain that produces a positive emotional state. Amphetamine and cocaine increase dopamine levels and while no one would argue using drugs like these to enhance skill or even just to study, the fact is that there is much we can learn about ourselves by studying some aspects of people who take them. To us, that highlights what is already known, that engagement and a positive attitude really help with learning. The question is how do we get these states naturally in higher education, and experiential education may help.

Now that is focus. Each act looked purposeful, but in the end it was not. The same basic, pointless repetitive behavior is also easily observable in animals given amphetamine. If a money incentive boosts the dopamine levels in the brain, and it does, that could explain our real-world sense that money is good at focusing behavior. But focus may not always be what we want. In motivating creative, high-performing people in creative industries, for example, we may want something money cannot buy.[21] In motivating artistic students in a university setting, we may want something that grades cannot inspire. Colleges and universities have designed their curricula and instructional systems to work for conscious learning. They have generally left adrift the unconscious learning that involves the many emotional brain circuits, a few of which have been discussed here. We leave the completion of a young person's education to the real world or the school of hard knocks, through jobs and other life experiences. But those direct real-world experiences, I argue, powerfully impact the unconscious decision-making processes of the mammalian brain, and thereby will shape our students' lives and careers in important ways.

So why do we in higher education leave that experience entirely outside of our scope, not addressed or complemented in the instructional program, left for after graduation? How can we fix our education systems to repair that neglect? Those questions will be addressed in the rest of this book by examining how experiential education works and can complement the classical academic curriculum.

---

21 Daniel Pink, 2011, *Drive: The Surprising Truth About What Motivates Us.*

Experiential Education Activities and

Implications

CHAPTER 7:

Internships

Of all of the experiential practices in higher education, internships can be the most powerful, if they are done properly. In this chapter, we will consider what it takes to construct an internship experience that is both effective and brain smart. I will also introduce two watchwords for gauging the quality of an experiential educational activity: "substantial" and "authentic." Both factors are important in having a strong, positive effect of an internship on student success.

In one of my last years as dean at Northeastern University, I helped lead a task force on experiential education, as part of developing a strategic plan for a new president. At that time, Northeastern was closing in on 100 years of cooperative education. At one of our task force meetings, a law school professor compared student learning in the law school's moot court activity with learning in an internship at a small law clinic—a type as part of their cooperative education program. He posed the question, which experience fostered learning that was the most substantial and most authentic?

As at virtually all law schools, moot court at Northeastern is a serious enterprise. Law schools typically have special rooms that look like a court. Students prepare intensively for their arguments, including dressing the part. Outside judges often are brought in to create an even greater impact.

To my surprise, the professor said that, for the individual student, the law clinic was the more powerful experience. Despite the attempts at realism in the moot court, he explained, everyone knows in the end that it is a student exercise. The law clinic, offering real work for real clients, is inevitably more authentic.

At the clinic, clients often depended on the students in real-world disputes. They thought of the interns as their legal guides, if not at quite the same level as the clinic's lawyers. Although the lawyers present the cases to the court, the students' work is typically an important part, and even though the interns were well supervised, if they missed something, the clients might be harmed. Those stakes made the clinic more authentic to the law students than the impressive but contrived high-drama of a moot-court exercise.

Turning to the term "substantial," the law professor explained that, at the clinic, students worked full-time alongside legal professionals. That was more substantial than a moot-court experience. Typically, internships were full-time for the entire term, following the hours of a real job after graduation. Years after law school, participants might still tell stories about the moot court, but their lives were more powerfully shaped by the clinic internships or other such intern experiences they had outside class.

Cooperative Education and Paid Internships

Cooperative education is essentially a paid internship that is full-time, term-long, and often repeated in the student's college education. It could be held at the same work site over the course of the student's college career, or at several different sites.

As mentioned already, cooperative education, in a formal sense, was first practiced in 1906 in the engineering program at the University of Cincinnati in Ohio. The innovator of the method was assistant professor Herman Schneider, who at a previous position at Lehigh University had observed that students with jobs outside the college often had a better approach to their studies in the classroom than those who lacked those work experiences. He developed the basic, simple framework for cooperative education of alternating classwork with industry work, but he left for Ohio in 1903 and implemented the program there, eventually becoming dean and then president at the University of Cincinnati. A statue of him is on that campus today.

In 1909, Northeastern University adopted the cooperative education model, followed about a decade later by Antioch University and Drexel University. Many other schools followed, and the model spread beyond engineering to business and other professional schools. Finally, in more recent years, the full model spread to the classic liberal arts and sciences programs at a few universities, although many arts and sciences students do internships, sometimes on their own.

The peak of cooperative education programs in U.S. universities began with a 1961 report from the Ford Foundation, "Work-Study College Programs: Appraisal and Report of the Study of Cooperative Education." In the wake of that report, the National Commission for Cooperative Education formed, which recently merged with the younger World Association of Cooperative Education, founded in 1983. From 1965 to 1992, the federal government, under the Higher Education Act, supplied funding to support cooperative education in the nation's universities. During that period some 150 colleges and universities took part, across a spectrum of fields and disciplines. Many of those programs stopped, however, with the end of federal funding. Today, educational institutions have started to renew interest in the concept, driven in part by the demand from industry to generate more work-ready college graduates, and in part by students, who often seek internships to try to gain experience to get the jobs they want.[1] Additionally, a broader public concern about the value and price of higher education (Blog Footnote 7.1)[2] factors into this discussion.

While a century-long history of cooperative education is impressive, the idea of learning through work is much older and more natural than most of us would think. Apprenticeships, for example, are a tradition that began in the Middle Ages, 1,500 years ago. Tied to craft guilds and sanctioned by governments, apprentice activities provided young people with food, lodging, and typically a poor salary, along with an opportunity to learn a craft by doing it. Being an apprentice was often the only way to enter the profession.

As many middle-schoolers learned, Benjamin Franklin studied the printing trade as an apprentice to his brother in Boston. An apprentice's life was hard, and Franklin famously ran away to Philadelphia. There, he set up his own printing business.

Apprenticeships worked because their goal was clear—a trade and a job—and they followed a well-understood path. The skills needed were clear, as was the supposed time of completion. To become a printer in Franklin's time, for example, one had to know how to set type, among other skills. Courses or training programs on that aspect of the profession did not exist; everyone learned at the elbow of a master. At the end of the traditional

---

1 Any online search will turn up such materials, but maybe start here: (http://www.usnews.com/news/articles/2015/05/05/study-suggests-college-graduates-benefit-more-from-paid-internships) or with this link within that article (http://burning-glass.com/research/internships-2015/)

2 Blog footnote 7.1 *From working class to classy work and beyond*, by Juliana Schatz and Jim Stellar, posted 4/10/10. http://otherlobe.com/from-working-class-to-classy-work-and-beyond/) This is a story of a student who discovered herself through cooperative education by working at a remarkable job with *Frontline* documentaries. That helped her to get into Columbia School of Journalism. She did not have to run away like Benjamin Franklin did, but her personal growth from the experience might have been just as substantial.

apprenticeship period, seven years in the case of a printer—other trades had different periods—the worker would be ready and accepted by the guild and the public as a printer. The apprentice system worked for Franklin, even though he impetuously took a shortcut in his apprenticeship.

The nineteenth century saw a gradual shift of most educational activities for young people out of the workplace and into the classroom. Lecturers and books became the preferred method of education, pushing the role of experience to the margins as an extracurricular activity. Apprenticeships came to be relegated to the trades, and the power of learning from direct experience was too often forgotten or downplayed in the operation of classic ivory-tower higher-education institutions. Formal accreditation of colleges and universities, which began at the beginning of the twentieth century, further marginalized the apprenticeship. Accrediting agencies judged higher-educational institutions primarily by the quality of their classroom-based curricula and the strength of their faculty.

But there are fields that were exceptions to this trend, such as medical education. One cannot practice as a medical doctor without completing an internship, and most likely a residency. Medical educators and practitioners clearly believe that a person needs to have practiced what was learned in medical school before being considered a full-fledged doctor. Today's medical-school curriculum even involves bringing some clinical experiences into the first few years rather than the old way of teaching overwhelmingly classroom material for the first two years.

The same is true in other professions beyond the health sector. Architects must work in the field before they can sit for the license exam. Teachers go out for a practicum, often in their last year of college, before they get their undergraduate degree and their initial certification. Yet, so many college students earning an undergraduate degree today are required to do nothing in their chosen fields, beyond taking classes. If they do gain any practical experience, it is often on their own.

If accreditation contributed historically to moving colleges and universities away from relying on direct experience in potential professions, maybe the trend is reversing today due to a recent emphasis by accrediting agencies on assessing what a student has learned, rather than just on what the faculty has taught. This trend fits with other trends in higher education that put the student at the center. For example, universities are creating more active learning opportunities in the classroom by having instructors move from being what is called a "sage on the stage" to more of a "guide on the side." Online learning often includes elements that are self-paced as students develop requisite skills before proceeding to the next step as in the Khan Academy,[3] or focus of the American Academy of Colleges and Universities on high impact practices.[4] As the focus shifts to the student, the distinction between curricular and extra-curricular learning becomes less important. It is all about the student's growth.

As mentioned in the first chapter of the book, I learned the value of experience-based learning firsthand, many years ago, in the summer after my own undergraduate junior year of college, when I worked in a neuroscience research laboratory. I felt that I learned as much about biology there, without getting any academic credit, as I did in my formal biology classes. I learned something else from my summer internship experience: I wanted to be a part of that field. In the following years, students who worked in my lab have told me they had similar realizations. Maybe that is why from the very beginning of my research career, even as a graduate student, I have always had undergraduates around me in the laboratory. Why shouldn't they have the opportunities that I did?

Some Classical Models of Cooperative Education

The basic principles underlying cooperative education have not changed since Herman Schneider's time. A student leaves the classroom for

3 https://www.khanacademy.org
4 https://www.aacu.org/leap/hips

a paid experience at a work site, where she works alongside others who are part of that profession. The site varies and could be a large company, a small mom-and-pop shop, a non-profit, or a research laboratory. It is most likely off campus, but could be on campus as long as it is real career-based work that is being done by the student.

In such an environment, all that really matters is what you the student can do. Of course, that depends partly on your formal knowledge, but you are assessed not by regurgitating it on a test but by applying it—using it for real work. You need to fit into the culture of the place and to interact with the knowledge of the field.

A cooperative education experience can have a powerful effect, even if it is sometimes hard to describe. Students grow up; and they are aware of that growth and often are proud of it. (Blog Footnote 7.2)[5]. Sometimes they change their planned career path and take different courses when they return to college. We see that they also find a new appetite for the rest of their academic curriculum and consume it in a more vigorous and deliberate way, just as one would expect from a more mature person.

The length of the experience does not matter so much as its authenticity. Cooperative education generally is conducted over the course of a term at most universities or even a six-month period overlapping the summer, as currently practiced at Northeastern University. The experience does need to be substantial to have a powerful impact. I do not think working just a few weeks over a spring break, or part-time during the semester, can deliver the same experience. Short experiences have value, but an immersion in the environment is important, and that takes time.

Any job supervisor knows that a new employee goes through a natural period of adjustment before mastering the job. The same goes for students. I could see the adjustment in students who worked in my laboratory on a

5 Blog footnote 7.2 *The Undergraduate Experiential Education of an MBA*, Corinne Freeman D'Ambrosio and Jim Stellar, posted on 10/23/11 (http://otherlobe.com/the-undergraduate-experiential-education-of-an-mba/). Corinne was an anthropology major who wound up in business with an MBA. In this post she reflects on lessons learned from her cooperative education experience and how it would later serve her in business. The backward judgment in time of an educational experience from the perspective on an ongoing career is particularly important to seeing the value of such an experience.

six-month cooperative education period. Employers involved in cooperative education outside the university environment tell me that their experience with students is no different.

The student's rise in mastery is very important to their growth. A key threshold is when they begin to think of themselves as regular employees and are seen that way by the other workers. By then, the student typically has a work station, has fit into the office culture, knows the others as colleagues, has assigned duties that are real, is treated with respect, and gets paid.

And often, when these students finish their stint in the workplace and return to the classroom full time, they have to get used to being students again. I have seen this adjustment from the unusual perspective of being both a cooperative education employer for a research laboratory on campus, and a faculty member who has had his former student-employees in a class in the next term. Cooperative education employers have an adjustment, too. After a student has spent six months working as one of our laboratory technicians, we might ask in the next week, "Why isn't John here today? Oh, yeah, he's back taking classes again." Some cooperative education students even get hired back part time in the following semester.

Pay is another very important factor in student growth. Remuneration makes the entire process more serious, from the very first day. With money in the game, employers are less likely to assign students menial tasks, such as fetching the proverbial cup of coffee. The students typically feel more committed to the arrangement. It may be the first time they have ever been paid for work other than baby-sitting or lawn-mowing. More important, the students usually feel an obligation to pay attention in training and to try to please coworkers, because they are more aware of the possibility of getting fired. Plus, they are pleased to have money.

It was interesting for me, as a college professor, to see cooperative education students come back to the residence hall at 6:30 PM, sometimes in business attire, not having any homework that night but having money to go out with friends. Of course, the co-op student has to get up and go to work the next day; it's a real job.

Another important feature of the cooperative education experience is the relevancy of the job to the student's major field of college study. One can grow up from any experience. I learned a great deal about myself on a surfing trip in 1970 with two buddies after our sophomore year of college. We drove a van from Philadelphia to southern California and up and down the coast. That summer I got better at surfing, grew up some, but I did not learn much that I could put toward my biology major or my later career.

As a professor, I knew that many students working in my research laboratory wanted to go to medical school, but they liked learning how scientists actually made the discoveries that underlie medicine. Some of them wanted to combine such research and practice. A few students wanted to be pure scientists. All of them became convinced that their laboratory work was relevant. I detected the same conviction in economics majors who worked in banks and pre-law students of various majors who worked in law firms. A significant side benefit was that their work supervisors could write strong letters of recommendation, as I could for students who worked in my lab. I noticed that applicants to medical school who had worked in a laboratory had quite a leg up, when they could elicit letters from university professors and hospital physicians who had supervised them full-time outside of class. The same happened in other fields.

Even if the cooperative education experience did not work out and a student discovered that the profession was not for them, it was valuable. Many students have expressed gratitude to me that cooperative education saved them from wasting time and money in graduate or professional school preparing for a job they would have hated. A typical comment from one of these students was: "My mother said I should be a lawyer because I was good at arguing, but on my last co-op term the work in the law firm felt like reading a dictionary, and the lawyers were always one-upping one another."

Those realizations were valuable, but I especially liked hearing the converse: "The law is like the Rosetta Stone of social justice, and lawyers are like clergy translating it for the people. Now I know I want to be an international human rights lawyer and fight against human trafficking. I am adding more language and some international relations courses to my history major, and I will possibly study abroad in Southeast Asia for a term to get experience out of my country before going to law school." Now what professor wouldn't want to teach a student like that one—someone on fire with passion based on a solid experience? Such a student would raise the academic level of any class.

Also not to be underestimated are the social influences upon students in a work setting. In the workplace most people are older than college students and have been there for a while. The student has to fit in or face real consequences. One may retake a course if one fails the final, but if the student fails to fit into the office culture or, worse yet, fails a client, the company could lose its business and people could lose their jobs. Social scientists Etienne and Beverly Wenger-Trayne and other scholars have a whole line of research on "communities of practice,"[6] such as an office where professionals share a common language, a way of doing things, and a purpose for being there. Students in cooperative education learn to navigate in these workplace communities of practice, something they do not get in the college classroom.

As mentioned in the beginning of this book, what is called cooperative education in the United States goes by "work-integrated education," or WIL, in many European universities and national organizations such as the Australian Collaborative Education Network[7]. WIL reflects the basic arrangement of integrating work with learning and thus the term may be a less mysterious term than cooperative education. However, I do like the idea of cooperation between the workplace and the academic institution that comes to me whenever I hear the term. A highly

6 http://wenger-trayner.com
7 http://acen.edu.au

specialized variation of this model is the German version that happens at the Baden-Württemberg Cooperative State University. Here, the student is hired as an actual employee of a company and admitted to the university at the same time, making the two entities complete partners in the student's focused education. Still, many universities in the United States and Canada stand by the term cooperative education.

Externships and Sandwich Programs

At the Culinary Institute of America, or CIA, students can take a 15-week externship program that comes in the middle of the two-year associate's degree program. It is a one-time experience for academic credit; it may be paid or unpaid, and it is intense. In fact, the whole experience at the CIA, as they like to call themselves, is intense. Students can take a variety of externship positions but normally work in the commercial kitchen, sometimes, perhaps at the restaurant of a CIA graduate. The CIA externship manual lays out a well-defined set of requirements for students to follow, including that students document their experience weekly in various ways. Externship supervisors meet with the student weekly and sign the record of the work completed in the externship manual. One CIA faculty member told me that the experience helps students translate "fundamentals into professionalism."

Externships generally are shorter than cooperative education experiences and are the preferred route at professional schools that are highly focused on careers. At some institutions, externships are hard to distinguish from cooperative education. In the past, Johnson & Wales University, for example, has used the two terms interchangeably. They even organize externships outside the food industry in business, technology, counseling, psychology, and education.

Another variant, found mostly outside the United States so far, is called a "sandwich program." It gives students repeated experiences working in industry in short periods or layers that alternate with layers of academic study. This work is typically paid. A 2012 report in the United Kingdom suggested that a greater emphasis be placed on sandwich programs, as they give students superior preparation for the workplace and are part of what Wilson calls the "supply chain to business."[8] I agree, and add that the same benefit is true for students seeking admission to any graduate program, but particularly those seeking a profession (e.g., a master's degree in journalism).

Unpaid Internships

Having covered the most substantial and authentic experiences—full-time, term-long, paid employment—we move to unpaid internships. Ross Perlin made the case against unpaid internships with a powerful 2011 book entitled *Intern Nation: How to Earn Nothing and Learn Little in the Brave New Economy.* Unfortunately, there are some companies or agencies that appear to accept interns but make little investment in training or compensating them. Some of these unpaid internships have been the subject of lawsuits, as an Internet search will reveal. The companies receiving that unfavorable spotlight appeared to not treat students as true apprentices; instead they may used them as free labor for the simplistic tasks, such as the classical stuffing envelopes or fetching coffee. Yes, observant and outgoing students may benefit simply from being in the work environment and in contact with the regular staff, and they can benefit from listing the experience on their résumé. But we, as a higher-education industry, can and must do better.

The question, as Perlin points out, is whether those benefits are worth the significant cost of the internship to the student, including living expenses and lost wages. If an internship is essentially required for a student to enter the profession, the lack of any pay creates a major issue of fairness. Are the company's doors only open for students who have the money to complete an internship without any pay?

---

8 *The Wilson Review,* 2012. (https://www.gov.uk/government/uploads/system/uploads/attachment_data/file/32383/12-610-wilson-review-business-university-collaboration.pdf)

A university that encourages or aids its students in taking unpaid internships should be aware that the unpaid intern has few legal employment rights. If subjected to mistreatment, such as harassment, at the company, the unpaid intern may be surprised to find that labor laws do not apply to unsalaried workers, and the recourse available to regular employees through the company's human resources department may not be available.

These and other concerns have led to some recent interpretations of the old 1938 Fair Labor Standards Act and a set of criteria that makes some companies wary of using unpaid interns. In response, these companies may ask for a letter from the university stipulating that the unpaid internship is part of the academic program and even credit-bearing. As a professor, I have occasionally supplied such letters, but only if the internship site clearly provided opportunities for learning. I required academic work such as a paper to be completed by the student, I asked for the employer's involvement in the evaluation, and I judged the work by the standards of a credit-bearing course. On the one hand, the great expansion of student interest in internships mean academic institutions have a responsibility to make sure internships meet high standards for learning, are done right, and abide by the modern interpretation of this labor law, especially if they are unpaid. On the other hand, we have the issue of faculty time and additional budget needs. As usual, such balancing between institutional forces requires careful on-campus discussions.

Some lessons from cooperative education programs can help universities navigate the waters of unpaid internships. One lesson is that the college and the company need to have a genuine partnership. The main risk with unpaid internships is that neither partner supervises the student's internship experience well enough, and the student learns little. Although either partner could take the lead, in my opinion, the university is the logical choice because it is focused on the student's education before, during, and after the internship. Cooperative education programs sometimes refer to this three-step sequence as preparation-activity-reflection. In my view, the academic institution should facilitate this cycle with all internships, whether paid or unpaid.

A long-term partnership between the college and any company or other organization that provides internships can be quite rich, with the exchange of important guidance on the preparation of students for the workplace.[9] (Blog Footnote 7.3). Students can carry back guidance to the college, as well—not only about the employer and their own learning, but also about the relevance and quality of the academic program. But to get that feedback, as well as to protect the student, the university must give full attention and make the student the first priority in the arrangement.

What about students who find internships on their own? That typically happens during summer break, but it also can happen during other periods like the short winter or January term break that some institutions have. For part-time internships, it typically occurs during the regular semester while the student is in classes. A student needs an academic plan to get the most educational value from an internship, though the plan can evolve and thus not have to be thought out completely in advance. At the very least, and in my opinion, it is the obligation of the career services operation to lead the college or university in forming such learning plans, and connecting students with faculty members or other subject matter experts.

Part-time Internships, Job Shadowing, Field Experiences

As discussed above, not all internships have to be full time. Students may find other types of experiences that, while less substantial and authentic, can be of great benefit to their growth and career development. The advantage to the college or university is that part-time internships can be less expensive to provide. The advantage to students is that part-time experiences may fit more easily into their busy lives. For those students

---

9 Blog footnote 7.3 This footnote refers to two blog posts. *An Internship in three phases.* Paulina Smietanka and Jim Stellar, posted 2/15/12 (http://otherlobe.com/an-internship-in-three-phases/) and *Internship number two – a growing experience.* Paulina Smietanka QC '14 and Jim Stellar (posted 8/13/12 (http://otherlobe.com/internship-number-two—a-growing-experience/). The first post has three supplemental parts that are included at the end of the chapter and makes a point about growth during an internship. The second post is all one and makes the point about growth between internships.

who must balance earning money to support themselves with a college education, a part-time internship may be all they can manage.

A student who is assisting a faculty member with a research project on campus is really doing a part-time internship. We know these experiences can be very valuable (Blog Footnote 7.4).[10] The same is true for service and service-learning programs, particularly if they are associated with academic courses. Ironically, due to the direct involvement of faculty, these kinds of on-campus part-time internships are often better integrated with rest of the student's education than the internship off campus, even though both should be. The key to this integration is reflection and we will come back to that in a later chapter.

Job shadowing, even if informal, can also be valuable. Many adults who did not do an internship in college got their first glimpse of a career during high school or even college, through a brief visit to a job site, perhaps arranged by a relative or family friend. Such experiences often plant the seeds of ideas about what to do with one's life. A simple job-shadowing experience can shape the choice of college major.

Because job shadowing has a brief timeline, it allows for multiple experiences, which can give a kind of breath to the student's appreciation for the field. The same is true for the provider of the experience, and that gives universities a way to reach out to alumni who are eager to help students from their alma mater but may not have the capacity to provide a job. Students love attention from the alumni network, and the college development office appreciates any deepening of the college's relationship with its alumni.

"The ultimate interview is an internship," is a line I frequently used to persuade a company to work with the university. It works with job shadowing. It works even better with internships. As a researcher who employed students on cooperative education or paid internships, I almost

11 Blog footnote 7.4 Internships and growth – one student's story, by Rachel Eager and Jim Stellar, posted on 7/27/15 (http://otherlobe.com/internships-and-growth-one-students-story/). This post looks at the high positive impact on her confidence in her freshman year by providing a place where she can do good work and grow as a result. Her work was in public health, but she generalized her experience to a research study done on a student-run public relations firm in another university.

always hired one my former undergraduate interns when I needed a full-time research technician. No one else could compete. The former interns had all the experience that I needed and I knew they could do the job. The same thing can apply to job shadowing, just not quite as strongly, since the bond between the student and provider may not be as developed. However, someone who has had several job-shadowing experiences may acquire valuable savvy from seeing a range of employers; presumably one can get better at speed dating as well.

Similar to job shadowing—but typically longer and often more substantial are field-experience programs organized by the university. Sometimes they function like unpaid internships; other times they are credit-bearing courses that send students out of the classroom to perform services in the field, which can be the community, a faculty research lab, or a business or other organization. Field experiences often take place during the short winter term, if the college has one. A three- or four-week period is a good length for the purpose.

One benefit of structure of the winter-term field experiences is the cross-fertilization that can happen when many students have different experiences at the same time, and can attend each other's term-end presentations before returning together to the spring term of classes. This is a powerful form of reflection, where students watch and sometimes judge each other's projects.

An attractive aspect of field experience programs, as mentioned in job shadowing, is the ability to involve alumni or local businesspeople with student entrepreneurship. A student may design a product or a service under the tutelage of a serious field expert, even right on campus. A January term is enough time for a serious, if brief, service experience abroad, for which a week-long spring break would not be enough. For example, many organizations will enroll students in medical missions and other humanitarian operations during winter term. When I was provost at

Queens College, a group of our drama students went to Athens during winter term and performed a newly written Greek narrative play. They returned to campus and in the spring term performed — as they carefully explained to me — the U.S. premiere, not the world premiere, which had already happened.

Back to the Brain

I began this chapter by contending that the most powerful of the experiential education activities are substantial and authentic. If done right, it is immersive. The student swims in it, absorbs the culture, develops his or her knowledge into professionalism. Some might say that an internship teaches both the emotional intelligence (i.e., the *emotional quotient*, or EQ) as well as the classical academic intelligence (i.e., the *intelligence quotient*, or IQ), components of the person (Blog Footnote 7.5).[11]

Good classrooms, with their syllabi and polished lecturers, may be the most efficient way to transmit large amounts of knowledge from an expert person to a group of learners. But the classroom cannot show as adequately the impact of knowledge on a real-world environment or on an enterprise in which other people depend on the learner making sense of that knowledge.

Immersion in a real-world experience triggers what has been referred to earlier as the mammalian brain, which employs unconscious or emotional brain-based decision making. The knowledge so acquired is *felt*, tacit knowledge, which can arouse the student's passion for a field of study, a process that *Talent Code*'s Coyle calls "ignition."[12] A student so roused puts much more time into his classroom studies, which of course improves

---

11 Blog footnote 7.5 *Internships in Law — EQ meets IQ processing*, by Hillary W. Steinbrook and Jim Stellar, posted 1/23/11 (http://otherlobe.com/internships-in-law—eq-meets-iq-processing/). We have a theory that an internship draws out the emotional intelligence, or EQ, processing and can allow it to be connected to the IQ type processing that is particularly seen in the law. In this post, we explore how one of the most revered institutions of education, Harvard Law School, profits from internships.

12 Daniel Coyle. *The Talent Code: Greatness Isn't Born. It's Grown. Here's How,* BantuamBantam Books, New York, NY, 2009.

his academic record, and also may change the processing in the knowledge circuits of the brain so the student can better use those facts and theories. In learning a skill, Coyle argues, one becomes faster in processing. As discussed in Chapter 6, the brain appears to be capable of re-wiring or re-mapping its functional areas, through long effort and over much time. That is, indeed, what Gladwell's outliers[13] do, once they become ignited in a specific field.

Maybe this enhanced processing becomes knowledge fluency. Whatever it is, it is good for students. It is natural for people. It is the oldest form of learning. And it is from experience. It may be the way our brains are built. It is nice for universities to give students a classroom-based introduction to a field before we engage in it; and classrooms, textbooks, and research papers are efficient ways of delivering knowledge to groups of people. The brain "learns by doing," a statement made by John Dewey, the famous educational reformer, in the first half of the twentieth century.

Think back to the question posed in the previous chapter: Why use only the primate portion of the brain, and not the mammalian portion, which evolved over millions of years and makes important unconscious decisions? Why not have the students try on the experiences of the career path they are exploring through their college major? Somewhere along the line, higher education forgot the role of experience. Now we know about the role of the hidden brain[14] in learning, or the brain that is incognito,[15] or the brain that thinks fast as well as slow.[16] It is time that we in higher education remember our John Dewey. That is what the fMRI machine and modern neuroscience are telling us.

---

13 Malcolm Gladwell. *Outliers: The Story of Success*, Little Brown and Company, New York, NY 2008.

14 Shankar Vedantam, *The Hidden Brain: How Our Unconscious Minds Elect Presidents, Control Markets, Wage Wars, and Save Lives.* Spiegel and Grau, 2010.

15 David Eagelman. *Incognito: The Secret Lives of the Brain.* Pantheon Books, New York, NY, 2012.

16 Daniel Kahneman, Thinking Fast and Slow, Farrar, Straus, and Giroux, New York, NY, 2011.

CHAPTER 8 :

Service and Service-Learning

Service and service-learning programs are perhaps the oldest forms of experiential education in U.S. colleges and universities. The idea of combining service and learning comes easily to these institutions, with their traditions of being not-for-profit and where both faculty members and students are often generous with their time and talents. When a student expresses the desire to serve others, my first thought is, "Here is a good person," but as an academic administrator, I also think next about the hyphen in service-learning. To me, the hyphen represents our challenge to connect the desire to serve with the college learning that will be important to students' continued development. As much as college administrators support pure service by campus clubs and other organizations and are proud of their contributions to the community, we perform our own mission for students best when we link service experiences with learning (Blog Footnote 8.1).[1]

I doubt there is a classical college or university in America that doesn't provide service opportunities for its undergraduates. And many outside organizations are there to assist. Campus Compact, for example, boasts 1,200 college campus members in more than 30 states. Campus Compact reported in 2011 that over 90 percent of its members describe service expressly as part of their mission statements. For example, the motto of Queens College CUNY, where I worked, is *"Discimus ut Serviamus,"* Latin for "We learn so that we may serve." I always liked to turn that around and say, "We also serve so that we may learn." The institution where I currently work, University at Albany SUNY, just began a public engagement operation[2] that will include working on complex societal problems and documenting what work faculty and others do in this area. The point is that there is much our students and our universities can take for their own growth and development by being of service, in addition to all they can give.

The 1980s saw a surge in service programs on campuses and a similar surge in support organizations. Besides Campus Compact (1985), national service organizations founded in that period include the National Youth Leadership Council (1982), the Campus Outreach Opportunity League (1984), the National Association of Service and Conservation Corps (1990), and Youth Service America (1986). The decade ended with a federal law, the National and Community Service Act of 1990 creating the Commission on National and Community Service.[3]

Many off-campus direct service organizations also began at this time. For example, City Year was launched by two former Harvard Law School roommates, Michael Brown and Alan Khazei in 1988. Their goal

---

1 Blog footnote 8.1 *A Service Experience and an Expectation,* by Adrienne Dooley and James Stellar, posted on 2/22/09 (http://otherlobe.com/a-service-experience-and-an-expectation/). A new freshman student's experience with a new service program designed to build community service while acquainting students, in this case, with the idea of serving the homeless as college students.

2 http://www.albany.edu/outreach/definitions.php

3 For more history of federal involvement, see the Corporation for National and Community Service web site (http://www.nationalservice.gov/about/legislation).

was to offer young people an opportunity to give a year of service in an urban environment, either before or after college. More than twenty-five years later,[4] it has spreadto more than twenty-six city locations in America as well as international sites. After the Obama administration asked City Year to focus on helping secondary schools with low graduation rates, the program shifted course, and developed a presence in about one-quarter of the failing high schools in the United States, with thousands of volunteers.

Teach for America,[5] another off-campus direct service initiative, trains recent college graduates to be teachers and places them in public schools that serve disadvantaged populations of students. The program grew out of founder Wendy Kopp's 1989 senior honors thesis at Princeton University. Launched with 500 volunteers in 1990, it has grown to well over 30,000 people and spread across the nation to become the most prominent volunteer program to address educational needs in the United States.

AmeriCorps, Engineers Without Borders, and Global Brigades are a few more examples among many service organizations with which colleges and universities can partner with to promote service-learning. You can find more online. Finally, the classic teacher-preparation programs in colleges and universities help to bring higher-education students of all types into contact with K-12 education. That and the similarities of educational mission gives rise to many local programs often created by students. Once these programs are created, they offer further development in partnership, such as internships, and that strengthens the university's ability to deliver opportunities its students want, and to facilitate students as they learn about themselves.

Serious Service-Learning and Community Service

In 2014, *U.S. News & World Report* published a list of 20 universities

---

4 http://www.cityyear.org and more specifically http://www.cityyear.org/sites/default/files/AR2014finalLR-July2015-NameEdits.pdf
5 https://www.teachforamerica.org

where college administrators were "mentioned most often" for "stellar examples of service learning."[6] It's not surprising to me that many schools on that list were also highly ranked in overall in the magazine's general lists.

The service-learning standouts do not fit a single mold. For example, they vary in size from small to large, ranging from 1,200 to 22,000 undergraduates; they have endowments of from $42 million to $5 billion. One key feature that most have in common is having a dedicated center for service-learning. Many of them are among the 240 U.S. institutions to be classified by the Carnegie Foundation for the Advancement of Teaching as "Community Engagement Campuses," for which a strong service-learning program is a key requirement.

Some have incorporated service into their fundamental structure, for example, by making it part of what can be counted in the faculty tenure process. Clearly, these colleges all have a long-term commitment to service-learning that has become woven deeply into the fabric of everyday campus life. An Internet search[7] turns up no shortage of information, best practices, and models for people looking to find ways to increase their institution's commitment to service-learning.

A Popular Campus Trend

Popular ideas in academia, and elsewhere, can be spotted by the

---

6 In alphabetical order, the 2014 list is: Berea College, Brown University, Butler University, College of the Ozarks, Duke University, Elon University, Georgetown University, James Madison University, John Carroll University, Loyola University Maryland, Michigan State University, Northeastern University, Portland State University, Stanford University, Tulane University, University of Michigan-Ann Arbor, University of North Carolina-Chapel Hill, University of Pennsylvania, Wagner College, and Warren Wilson College. Source: http://colleges.usnews.rankingsandreviews.com/best-colleges/rankings/serving-learning-programs (form 3/20/2015).

7 Among a few relevant websites I found in 2015 are:

- Guides to programs (http://evergreen.loyola.edu/rcrews/www/sl/academic.html,) or studies by the Higher Education Research Institution at UCLA and other groups.

- Documentation on all forms of service-learning is available at the National Service Learning Clearing House (http://www.servicelearning.org/). One can find organizations

- Organizations that promote service-learning, such as the American Associate of Community Colleges. (http://www.aacc.nche.edu/Resources/aaccprograms/horizons/Pages/default.aspx) or the Corporation for National and Community Service (http://www.nationalservice.gov/).

- Conferences exist. (http://servicelearningconference.org/).

- Foundations that specialize in service issues like Bonner (e.g. http://www.bonner.org/) include or historically the Carnegie Foundation, which maintains a Community Engagement list. Among relevant websites (e.g. http://evergreen.loyola.edu/rcrews/www/sl/academic.html) or studies by the Higher Education Research Institution at UCLA and other groups.

appearance of a thicket of related book titles, and many books have been written on service-learning in the past couple of decades. For example, a famous one from 1999 is by Janet Eyler and Dwight E. Giles' *Where Is the Learning in Service-Learning?* A quick search on Amazon.com today will bring up a list of about fifty on the subject.

Service and service-learning programs also serve a number of purposes in higher education. Some admissions departments regard service programs as a lure for recruiting idealistic young students. Some administrators promote them as part of their institution's contribution to the community. Faculty members, who teach service-learning courses, and who, with advisors, help students interpret their service experiences say they observe a real growth in students' maturity and focus when they return from such a program. I've seen that growth, myself.

In spring 2014, while I was still at the City University of New York, the CUNY Service Corps[8] held its first celebration of students and service-site providers at the end of the first year of the program. I attended the conference, as I had been involved in the original set up of the program. The event brought together hundreds of students who had completed part-time, paid service internships. The students at each agency made brief poster-based presentations about the work they had done, and their accounts made a powerful impression on the attendees. I was impressed by the participating students' evident maturity, but I had already seen this effect before from my earlier experience with the cooperative education program at Northeastern University. The CUNY program's leaders were gratified to see that their program had such a broad and positive impact in the city. It was my impression that they were a bit surprised at how well students had performed and it is my feeling that, as this program continues to roll out over the following years, they, too, would come to expect this growth in their students.

---

8 http://www1.cuny.edu/sites/servicecorps/

The CUNY program is a good case for what is called a *high-impact practice*[9] for student success, to use a current higher-education buzzword phrase. High-impact practices are typically aimed at retention, keeping students from leaving college before they complete their degree. It works. More broadly, evidence exists that serious service-learning experiences can boost student success after graduation. For example, a 2014 Gallup-Purdue University poll[10] identified people who were highly engaged in their careers and asked them what college experiences had contributed to their success. Respondents who had completed a service project lasting more than one semester (like the year-long CUNY Service Corps) were more than twice as likely to say they were highly engaged at work as compared to other respondents. If that finding is valid, the students at CUNY's year-end conference not only should be better retained at college, but they likely also received a boost toward a successful career after graduation.

Service Abroad

In a fairly new wrinkle, many colleges offer service opportunities combined with their abroad programs, which can be primarily for study or expressly for direct service. Students who enter these programs—often those in developing countries— typically do not earn a wage. Unfortunately, that may put the programs beyond the reach of students who need paid work to afford tuition. For a student who can volunteer, many find it incredibly rewarding to spend time, for example, in a local village, helping people gain access to clean water, sanitation, or education.

This service need not take place during the student's college career, of course. Some college graduates deliberately take a gap year before or after college to do service or try a profession before going on to graduate school. Some students also just need a break from what has been a lifetime of schooling. These service experiences matter to students and leave them with

---

9 http://nsse.indiana.edu/html/high_impact_practices.cfm or https://www.aacu.org/leap/hips
10 http://www.gallup.com/poll/168848/life-college-matters-life-college.aspx

a personal maturity from the practice. If America had a year of national service between college and high school, it would be a positive benefit to our higher educational system.

Reflective Service

A larger role for service-learning should feel natural in our universities, given their ancient origins in monasteries. Those academic robes we professors wear at graduation are remnants of that monastic tradition, as is learning coupled with service. Monasteries were also places of reflection, which supports the modern adoption of reflective practices as an important part of the service-learning experience. Students who take part in a service activity in college are usually required to write a paper related to the experience. A paper, or another integrative exercise, is a way to help the student draw understanding from the experience in a scholarly format that a professor can review and grade. Many service-learning courses have such requirements, but I believe colleges and universities could do much more to integrate outside service-learning courses with academic study.

In one study in 2009, Janet Eyler of Vanderbilt University described a set of students who completed a full-time service-learning project followed by a capstone course, which is designed to bring together key aspects of a major in an academic discipline. The students were majors in human and organizational development. During their full-time service internships, they had returned to campus every week for a full day of reflection.[11] That day, they spent away from the work site, ate into their service time, but it was designed to help them integrate their service experiences with academic learning. Eyler's study found that such reflection improved the students' service experience dramatically and gave them a much greater appreciation for the activity and how it fit with their education.

---

11 2009, Janet Eyler of Vanderbilt University presented a paper at a conference at Clark University on "Liberal Education and Effective Practice." (http://www.clarku.edu/aboutclark/pdfs/eyler%20final.pdf)

The value of regular periods of substantive reflection carries over when the students go back to the service experience. They are armed with a greater awareness and capacity, resulting in a higher level of work and stronger engagement. Service and reflection can thus form a virtuous cycle, as David Kolb proposed in a theory of learning in 1984. He suggested that students have an experience, extract knowledge and theories from it, apply them to the next experience, and keep repeating. Such a cycle also fits well with theories about the role of repetition in learning, going back to the 1950s. Recall Donald Hebb, who said that, "Neurons that fire together, wire together." In metaphorical terms, we need the student's learning from the discipline they study in the classroom to "wire together" with their experiences in the field

In addition to deeper more integrated learning from the service experience or the internship discussed in the last chapter, another important goal of the experience-reflection cycle is to inspire the student.   As mentioned, this is the "ignition point" that Daniel Coyle described in *The Talent Code* -the point where a student commits to the field of study, or maybe does the opposite and changes fields because the commitment is not there. I believe that any higher educational institution, or unit within one, that aspires to have service projects bring students to that ignition point must commit fully to the concept of service-learning, internship, or whatever experiential activity they are offering. They must make the activity part of the academic major and enlist large numbers of students in it to create a positive social influence as well as a strong individual experience. Only then will the experience become an institutional high-impact practice and broadly engage the passion of the students.

Diversity

Most colleges and universities want to attract and hold diverse populations of students. College communities believe, rightly, that the quality of the education is higher if students and professors can draw upon the perspectives of a culturally and ethnically diverse population. Not surprisingly, an orientation toward diversity marries well to a strong mission of service-learning and diverse community service, particularly in urban universities. Such practices may even encourage attendance from diverse groups in that community and may encourage students from these groups to do better in college, as the university is seen as more welcoming to and understanding of students from outside the majority culture and ivory tower (Blog Footnote 8.2).[12]

In the 2000s, when I was the dean of the College of Arts and Sciences at Northeastern University—a period rapid rise in the university's reputation—everyone was celebrating the growth in scores, grades, and geographic spread of applicants for admission. Yet, some other administrators, as well as at least one group of students, noticed that fewer and fewer minority students from Boston-area high schools were naturally being enrolled. The students developed the idea that the university could try to reverse that trend by sending some of our students who were from Boston to visit their former high schools and encourage them to attend college in general. The student-led recruitment effort was named LEAD, for Linking Education and Diversity and, at the time, the admissions department at the time was very receptive. Eventually, the university contributed scholarship money and, for a time, turned LEAD into a full-blown student service program. Upperclass students ran the program with the support of admissions and the dean's office. Some of the student leaders even went on to work in university admissions, or became successful professionals, entrepreneurs, and so on. I saw firsthand how the program benefitted the LEAD students participants by being of service to the university and taking up the cause of diversity.

---

12 Blog footnote 8.2 *Inspiration is key to students from underrepresented groups*, by Tamara Buchanan and Jim Stellar, posted on 2/16/10 (http://otherlobe.com/inspiration-is-key-to-students-from-underrepresented-groups/). This post describes from a minority-student perspective what matters in motivating underrepresented groups to perform. It is one part inspiration from role models and one part inspiration from doing it yourself, either organizing a conference or studying abroad.
Also see the EOP program at the University of Albany as a programmatic example (http://www.albany.edu/eop/).

Don't Hurt Your Friends with Good Intentions

Before a university proposes a partnership with an outside service organization, the planners should put themselves in the position of their potential partner, just as cooperative education programs do with companies which support paid internships. What do these service partners need to sustain their efforts? In brief, the student participation should be set up in a way that serves the service provider, as well as the students and the university.

This is a lesson learned the hard way by every university I've served or worked with. For example, administrators initiating a new service-learning course will typically schedule it for the spring or fall semester but not both semesters at once and not over the summer. This plan may be convenient for the university but it is highly inconvenient to the service provider who needs assistance year-round.

If one is using academic courses to drive service-learning, the best approach is to start by teaching two such courses, one in each term and also by having some activity over the summer. The continuity of the supply of students will form the basis for a good partnership on many levels. The student experience will deepen as the partner begins to count on their work. Both the university and the service provider can continuously adjusted the practice to insure that each institution benefits now and in the future. Faculty can learn new things about teaching from consistently working with a service provider partner whose staff often has similar intellectual backgrounds as well as rich contemporary real-world experience. Faculty members may discover that the service partner opens up new avenues for academic research or opportunities to apply for grants; the service partner, in turn, may benefit from faculty research and analysis in their operation. When both partners as well as the students benefit, that is a partnership that has a chance of lasting.

CHAPTER 9:

Study Abroad

Study abroad is a third form of experiential education we have considered, in addition to the two previous chapters on internships and service-learning. If it is true that three points make a pattern, then with this chapter the experiential education pattern should emerge.

When I became the dean of the College of Arts and Sciences at Northeastern University in 1998, I inherited the college's small but robust study-abroad program. The previous dean, who founded the program, believed that study abroad should fundamentally be an academic experience. He also said, with respect to the university, that study abroad, internships, service-learning, and undergraduate research (which we will discuss in the next chapter) all fit under the umbrella of experiential education. I concurred, on both points. The umbrella concept was very useful at the time in convincing colleagues that those approaches should all be integrated into the conventional academic curriculum of an arts and sciences college.

When I took office, Northeastern's study abroad program had just a few hundred students, but it was a new and exciting offering. It was also fun for a college administrator to manage: I met interesting new people and negotiated partnerships with universities all over the world. Of course, that meant some travel.

The partner university would supply foreign teaching venues and housing for our students. In places where we could not enlist a university, we formed affiliations with other organizations to be local contacts and to help our students navigate the local circumstances.

One of the best parts of building the program in those days was seeing the growing interest of students in overseas study. Students found the experience fun, while it also gave them a different worldview from the students who did not study abroad. Other faculty members and I found it satisfying to see our students' resulting growth in maturity. Students returning to campus from abroad sold their peers on the program. Each year, its numbers grew. That mirrored what was happening nationally, where participation in study abroad climbed from around 50,000 students per year in the 1980s to almost 300,000 in 2012, according to the National Association of Foreign Student Advisers, which is now known as NAFSA: Association of International Educators.[1] Study abroad is now a major activity on many American campuses with its own interesting history from the turn of the twentieth century.[2]

---

1 http://www.nafsa.org
2 Another reason study abroad is so popular in the United States is the impetus from an historic internationalization movement that is about as old as cooperative education or service-learning themselves. The Institute of International Education, for example, was founded in 1919 to encourage U.S. citizens to go abroad. It enjoyed relationships with the U.S. State Department and the World Bank, the Ford Foundation, among other influential organizations. For decades, such organizations have encouraged universities to develop abroad programs, although some places didn't need any urging to do so. At the end of the 19th century, a few Indiana University professors invited their students to attend summer courses in a handful of countries in Europe. By the 1920s, the University of Delaware invented the junior year abroad, which spread to elite colleges until it was suspended during World War II. Study abroad recovered after the war and has surged since the late 1960s. Today, at some universities--especially elite private institutions--the question is when and where—and not whether—a student will study abroad.

Some student populations are typically reluctant to study abroad. Pre-medical students are one of them. This is a group I know well, as I was pre-med in college. Pre-meds often have eschewed overseas trips because they face such a tight set of curricular requirements for medical school. But with the addition of medical mission trips abroad to provide health services, pre-med students are starting to participate. Similar offerings have been well-received by majors in engineering and other applied fields with a tight curriculum, and many of them are studying abroad too, or at least going abroad while in college.

Follow the Money

Student popularity alone would be insufficient to make study abroad the success that it has become. It also requires the buy-in of administration and faculty to launch these programs. Historically, college administrators found study abroad programs easy to approve, as the work involves the same credit-bearing courses as the curriculum on the home campus with the same basic processes for course approval, accreditation, and transfer of course credit as at a domestic university. In addition, the partnership agreements between the home and foreign institutions can ensure that the courses have all the expected ancillary services, such as advising, housing, and even maybe access to a gym. Often the student need only select the desired foreign institution and find appropriate courses, often taught in English, and sign up.

And then there's money. For private U.S. universities, study abroad makes good economic sense. Most foreign universities are public and have a much lower tuition rate. Going abroad, the U.S. student pays the tuition at the home university and the home university can pocket the difference. At Northeastern, during my time as dean, the central administration allowed the college to keep the tuition dollars to support the program. Armed with that revenue, my office could afford to make the basic arrangements for our students to go abroad, even providing scholarships for travel where our students could not afford the plane tickets. Eventually, the program spread and moved up one administrative level to the provost's office, where it could have more of a university-wide role. Technically, there was an imbalance in budgeting: The tuition dollars spent on foreign study were not funding salaries and costs on the home campus. But both recruitment and retention improved and that helped the bottom line. Besides, to be competitive in the modern world, universities and colleges have to offer study abroad.

After I left Northeastern for the public-university world in 2009, I found that study abroad did not always ride on the crest of the economic incentive described above. Queens College CUNY, as a public university, had a tuition rate that was wonderfully affordable—wonderful, that is, for its students but not so good for funding its study abroad program. Because the tuition gap with foreign universities was small at best, Queens had little financial benefit from sending its students to study abroad. The program relied on the basic budget, and even charged a fee on top of tuition to meet expenses. There was really no extra revenue to help pay for students' plane tickets or housing in the foreign country.

But Queens had another resource: the generosity of its alumni and donors, who knew that it had deserving students who did not have the resources to take a term abroad without additional support. This included students who needed to work while to pay their tuition or support their families; they may not have been able to do without that income, even for a term. Donors were beginning to step up to fund travel scholarships, so deserving students were not denied important experiences that were commonplace at private universities. At Queens, in fact for a time, I was told by our development office at one point that donations for students to go abroad was only surpassed by funds raised for students to serve the community.

Another source of revenue that we are contemplating at the University at Albany, where I am now provost, is to increase the number of foreign students who come to our university to study abroad. That generates out-of-state tuition dollars that are higher than what in-state students pay. The difference could be applied to help public university students go abroad. It is also important to note that having students from other countries on campus increases the interest of domestic students in studying abroad. Friendships between foreign and domestic students drive learning and broaden the domestic students' worldviews without their even leaving campus.

Reflection

Getting students to embark on abroad experience is crucial, of course, but getting them to reflect on what they are doing can be an even greater challenge. One feature of those early days of study abroad at Northeastern was to get participating students to reflect on what was happening during their overseas adventure. Student reflection, we knew, was the key to their deeper processing of the experience (Blog Footnote 9.1).[3] We needed to turn tacit knowledge into explicit understanding and thereby have a greater impact on the student's college lives and studies. Without this deeper processing, the abroad experience is in danger of becoming just academic tourism.

To encourage reflection back in the Northeastern study-abroad program, we initially asked students to keep a journal of their experiences abroad. We first had them read a short guide to journaling called *Charting a Hero's Journey* by Linda Chisholm.[4] Students were supposed to follow the

---

3 Blog footnote 9.1 *Impact is the Point in Study Abroad*, by Dawn Anderson and *Jim Stellar* Posted on 12/22/09 (http://otherlobe. com/impact-is-the-point-in-study-abroad/). The title of this post says it all. In this post, we talk about going outside the comfort zone of the student or what has been called the zone of accepted practice by introducing students to what we call controlled chaos. Overwhelmingly, if not in all cases, it works and the students grow and tell us so even years after they graduate.

4 Linda A. Chisholm, *Charting a Hero's Journey*, Infinity Press, West Conshohocken, PA 2000. This guide to the writing of a journal for college students engaged in study abroad, off-campus study, or service-learning was funded by a grant of NAFSA: Association of International Educators.

sequence of stages laid out in the book, dating their entries. Students had to submit the finished journal on their return. We did not ask them to submit entries during their time abroad, because in the early 2000s, unlike today, we did not generally trust the availability of the Internet abroad. To my surprise, many of the returning students admitted that they completed the journal on their laptops on the airplane back home, or shortly after they arrived. They backdated their entries. Some of these students told me that they hated the reflection assignment. Though I was disappointed, I appreciated their frankness.

Today, blogs and other forms of social media make a very different environment for communication. Some students blog about their overseas experiences without even being asked. Student writings often show good evidence of reflection and are helpful to other students, both those who are abroad and those who are considering going abroad to study. But there is another way and it is revealing.

Faculty-Led Study Abroad

By the time Northeastern's classical study abroad program was growing strong, we were also developing another type of abroad program: faculty-led trips as part of courses or even as an entire course itself. This development took advantage of the pair of two-month summer sessions that Northeastern had created when it changed from a quarter-based to a semester-based academic calendar.

For a faculty-led trip, one of our professors typically would lead the trip to the selected country, teach one course, and help us hire someone from a local university to teach a second course, rounding out the course-load for the summer term. The first important faculty-led abroad course was a trip to Cairo, led by a political science professor. That trip served as a model for our thinking and later became a key part of Northeastern's international affairs major, as well as other majors. That first course was on city planning, using Cairo as an example. The accompanying course was Arabic language, taught by a faculty member from the American University of Cairo.

By focusing on the country, its language, culture, or history, this arrangement fulfilled the new core curriculum requirement for experiential education at the College of Arts and Sciences. Those first courses were followed by a few others, and then the floodgates opened with faculty-led abroad courses by the dozen. Each set of courses included a focus on understanding the country. Students were not just taking unrelated courses in an exotic place, as can happen in study abroad. We called our program Dialogue of Civilization to contrast with a famous book at the time called *The Clash of Civilizations and the Remaking of World Order.*[5] Under the then-director of the international relations program, Professor Denis Sullivan, we even took students to Cairo, Egypt, to study city planning (his course) and Arabic for foreign language credit.   But there were soon many such courses all over the world.

As for the role of reflection in a faculty-led study-abroad program, those students reflected all the time. Despite our difficulty in inducing students in our standard study-abroad program to write in their journals, students in the faculty-led trips could not stop talking about what they were learning.

What about the faculty-led system bred reflection? I believe it was simply that the students were all in it together. They were a cohort, not just one student or a handful who were studying, relatively isolated, at a foreign university. They were a team of Northeastern students in a challenging and intriguing environment, even if they were being taught by one of our professors.

What's more, the team created its own teaching. One student to

---

5 Samuel P. Huntington, *The Clash of Civilizations and the Remaking of World Order*, Simon and Schuster, New York, NY, 1996.

whom I was a mentor went on that Cairo trip, just mentioned, as her first abroad experience. From our conversations before she left, I knew that she had the idea that the hijab, or headscarf, was confining to Muslim women. She returned with a very different perspective and chose to try to do her undergraduate thesis on the implications of the hijab. How did this student broaden her viewpoint? The answer was in the team of students talking to each other. Not only did my student herself speak to a variety of Muslim Egyptian women, using the beginning Arabic that she was learning in Cairo, but she also involved her Northeastern women friends in those conversations with the Egyptian women, especially because some of the Northeastern women had a better command of the language than she did. Her fellow students reflected with her on the practice of wearing hijab. Of course, they discussed in English, as they hung out in their rooms and over group meals. My point here is that a student's individual reflection morphed into a group process that was powerful and immersive.

We will see more of this group process later. As we will find, learning by reflection in a group is very natural for the brain, as much of our unconscious decision-making may have evolved in early human groups and leverages these social interactions.

Study-Abroad Inc.

The popularity of study abroad on campus has become a factor in the evolution of higher education as an industry. Today, large universities and small colleges alike have substantial offices to manage study-abroad programs. Admissions offices love using smiling student faces in exotic settings to encourage admitted students to enroll at their institution.

Some universities even have branch campuses abroad. Although there are great benefits to that strategy, it is expensive and tends to tie a campus to a particular world location and risks that student interests might shift. In some ways, the opposite strategy is to enlist an outside company that for a fee can arrange study-abroad experiences in many locations, regardless of an institution's presence. Finally, some students make the arrangements themselves. For example, I know one student at Queens College who simply called the foreign student office of a Turkish university and arranged to take a few courses there in the summer and have a place to live in the dormitory. They were happy to have him as an international summer student. Fortunately for him, we at Queens accepted the credits when he returned.

As with most things, especially where there is demand, some caution is also needed. For example, these arrangements can be complicated since they involve money.

All parties, sending and receiving institutions and any entities that are brokering that student flow, need to remember that we are supposed to be serving student educational growth. The secondary goals of improving international understanding, having attractive programs for prospective student recruitment, or even making money are just that—secondary. It is particularly incumbent on the sending colleges and universities to make sure that students' interests are served first. In the last five years, this whole field has become increasingly professionalized. One prominent, long-standing study-abroad organization mentioned before, NAFSA, wrote a code of ethics for itself.[6] It is very gratifying to see this basic form of experiential education become so heavily incorporated into the ways most universities operate.

Faculty-Led Abroad Trips

To return to faculty-led abroad programs, I want to point out that they vary in their details and follow a variety of models. For example, regarding faculty compensation, different institutions with summer

6 http://www.nafsa.org/About_Us/About_NAFSA/Leadership_and_Governance/NAFSA_s_Statement_of_Ethical_Principles/

programs may provide extra pay or accept summer teaching in place of a course the professor would teach during the academic year. Some colleges and universities hire dedicated instructors to teach their courses abroad.

Because the courses are approved by the home institution and taught by their faculty, there is no question of where they fit in the curriculum. There is also no question about the standards for content, or whether they count when all return. Other arrangements, such as classroom or facilities used at a foreign university, still have to be negotiated and there are many arrangements to be made either, by the faculty who teach the course or any teaching assistants who accompany them. There are also variations where the traditional weeklong spring break can be used as part of a course or a one-month winter term can be used to run one whole course.

As with conventional study abroad, there are independent organizations outside of colleges and universities that promote faculty-led trips. Students are always advised to check with their home university before signing up. They must do their homework.

I also should point out that the experience is not limited to college students. Alumni organizations host trips for their people, often with faculty members leading or giving lectures. Commercial organizations do the same with special trips that are often organized around themes involving faculty leaders. All of these factors increase the excitement on campus for study abroad. To my way of thinking, this form of experiential education is highly important for the students and for a country that must operate on a global stage.

Student Reintegration

What happens to students returning to campus from study abroad? Some students experience reverse culture shock (Blog Footnote 9.2).[7] As a

---

7 Blog footnote 9.2. *Re-entry from Abroad Programs – Culture Shock and What it Means,* by Ruth Wyshogrod and Jim Stellar, posted on 2/9/10 (http://otherlobe.com/re-entry-from-abroad-programs—culture-shock-and-what-it-means/). After returning from a term abroad in Israel, this student had a hard time readjusting to America. But she had an unusual condition that may have exacerbated the experience – she lived there for the first few years of her life.

dean I took more than a few calls from puzzled parents, especially if I knew them personally. Parents wanted to know why their son or daughter seemed to be struggling with our culture after returning to their old environment.

I would be tempted to launch into an explanation of the neuroscience of sensory adaptation in the brain—a change of which the returning student would be unaware. Consider basic sensory adaptation. Do you remember putting on your underwear this morning? You felt the fabric then; do you feel it now? Probably not. The brain focuses our attention on what is new, things that change, like that scary-looking dog coming around a tree when you are out for your morning walk. That dog could hurt you. You are unlikely to be hurt by your underwear, that is, if it hasn't hurt you already.

Adaptation can be pretty dramatic. During my graduate studies at the University of Pennsylvania, the other students and I learned about a sensory adaptation study by Hans Wallach, a professor at Swarthmore College. He had his students wear goggles containing prisms that shifted their visual spatial perception. The sideways shift goggles was enough so that when a student wearing the goggles first reached for a doorknob, he missed. After a period of consistently wearing these goggles and trying to reach for objects, the perception corrected. One student had done the experiment with goggles that reversed up and down. Reportedly, the student was walking across campus as it was snowing, when a friend asked how the goggle experiment was going. The student answered something like, "I wish you hadn't said that. I had adapted to them, but now that you mention it, I am aware that it is snowing up."

Also surprising was the fact that, after adapting to the goggles and removing them, the students had to re-adapt to normal vision. It happened quickly, but not before a few students reached for doorknobs to the other side of where they actually were. That anecdote may provide the best parallel to the student who has studied abroad returning to where the formerly familiar has become unfamiliar. When my oldest daughter some time ago in high school returned from a summer service trip of many weeks to a remote village in Ecuador, she was astonished at the grandeur of our local supermarket. She had been to it a thousand times before, but now she saw it differently.

But other changes in the brain of a student may be even more important. Remember our discussion in Chapter 7 about the unconscious decision-making process that guides how we reach conclusions about so many things, from purchases to biases? Remember in Chapter 5 where we talked about neuroplasticity in the brain and how one needs strong engagement to change how its circuits function? Well, there may be no form of experiential education that provides stronger engagement or that is more immersive than going to another country to study, live, and even work. More research is needed on how these automatic processes that we have called the mammalian brain are changed by such experiences, but it is a worthwhile area of investigation in higher education and one that I suspect will be very important to getting the most out of experiential education.

I tell the parents of students who are returning from study abroad to just relax. Their kid will need some time to adapt back to their old world. Let them talk about their experiences, but just be prepared that that they may want to do that long after most of us tire of the conversation. It is a sign of a new passion—like a new hobby or maybe like the parents themselves as a young couple with their first baby. What I do not tell them is that some of these brain circuit changes may be permanent, especially the ones that govern how students look at the world. But maybe a parent should not be surprised that college changes people, including their kid!

Exchanges

Of course, foreign students also study abroad by coming to the United States. They meet American students, some who want to study in the foreign students' country. That can lead to an exchange, whether arranged by an educational organization or university in partnership with an overseas institution. Sometimes the exchange happens by accident, out of a chance meeting on campus. Regardless of how it occurs, whether formal or informal, an exchange can be a powerful interaction for both students involved.

Today many students in China want to study in the United States, while many U.S. students want the reverse. Especially interesting at Queens College was the fact that we had so many Chinese-born students on campus, due to our proximity to Flushing, a New York City neighborhood that is home to one of the largest Chinese immigrant communities in the United States. That situation gave rise to the possibility of exchanging students who wanted to study in their country of origin, but who were now U.S. citizens. Those students would sometimes visit their relatives in China, but by setting up exchanges of study abroad and, especially, by coupling that with overseas internships, we could leverage the students' linguistic and cultural competencies to help them get post-graduation jobs, in, say, a global industry.

On the flip side of the exchange, foreign nationals bring an important kind of global diversity to the university, precisely because of the idea that they will go home afterward and work in their country of origin (Blog Footnote 9.3)[8]. Of course, some do aim to stay in the country in which they studied, but many return home, and it is an asset for a university to have alumni in the country of origin. Specifically, over time, successful exchanges can help the university establish a network that can support partnerships with government agencies, businesses, and other universities in years to come. There is much more that could be said about this topic, including a variety of vendors that help universities develop international

---

8 Blog footnote 9.3. *Exploring Two Worlds*, by Ute Wenkemann NU'11 and Jim Stellar, posted on 2/3/10 (http://otherlobe. com/exploring-two-worlds/). The idea of a foreign student coming to study abroad in the U.S. and then going from the host institution (Northeastern University) on a cooperative education placement in the U.S. presents an interesting definitional quandary as to whether it is co-op abroad, but it is also a powerful experience and one that can be replicated by sending American students to study and then work abroad as discussed in the next blog post in this chapter.

student populations, but that takes us away from the experience itself and I will stop here.

Study Combined with an Internship

Some American university students are able to combine study on a foreign campus with an internship at a workplace in the same city (Blog Footnote 9.4)[9]. A simple combination is to study in the fall and work in the spring, making the abroad experience last one academic year. Doing the study portion first gives the student time for greater learning of the language and local customs before work begins.

The work site usually will produce a much deeper command of the language, compared to a classroom where the student expects to always get a second or third chance to correct a mistake. At work, when the student takes a call from a customer, or when a colleague wants to discuss a project, the encounter is a serious matter, with real purpose and no make-up test. Incidentally, these students told me that having a paid internship abroad strengthens language skills and cultural knowledge even better than a homestay arrangement where the students live with families in the abroad country. Given the seriousness of the work environment, perhaps that observation should not surprise an experiential educator as the work site is both more substantial and more authentic in terms of a potential career.

---

9 Blog footnote 9.4. *Combining Study Abroad with Cooperative Education Abroad*, by Jill Abbott and Jim Stellar, posted on 7/6/09 (http://otherlobe.com/combining-study-abroad-with-cooperative-education-abroad/). Jill makes the powerful observation that after following a study term with a work term in France for an Indian-based company she was able to do "French on the phone" even if she still struggled with the jokes. But perhaps the greatest learning was not in language fluency, but in intercultural dialogue and her own growth as a person.

CHAPTER 10:

Undergraduate Research

Of the many forms of experiential education, undergraduate research is the one that has meant the most to me personally. My own stint as an undergraduate researcher led me to change my choice of career. In the summer before my senior year of college as a biology major, I worked in a neuroscience lab at another university studying the brain. This led me to drop my long-held goal of medical school. I applied only to PhD programs and ultimately became a professor in neuroscience. To put it simply, that summer I fell in love with the brain, and I realized that I only liked medicine.

Thus, I speak from personal experience when I attest to the benefits of doing research as an undergraduate. But to fully understand its power to impact a college education, I had to observe students in my own research laboratory. I caught a glimpse of that power when I was a graduate student and had a few undergraduates working with me. I saw it again when I watched over a group of students in my first laboratory at Harvard. But, I had to leave the Ivy League and enter a much more nationally representative university, in terms of ranking by *U.S. News & World Report*, and then I had to see those students succeed there just like my Harvard or Penn undergraduates did. Only then did I really understand how undergraduate research could transform any student's career. The two words I have used previously— "substantial" and "authentic"—can be applied fully to undergraduate research, even if the student never leaves campus to do it.

Roots in UROP

Many professors who practiced undergraduate research in the late 1970s and 1980s took inspiration and ideas from the MIT's Undergraduate Research Opportunities Program (UROP), which began in 1969.[1] There had been earlier programs to encourage undergraduate research, such as the Sigma Xi honor society, which had been giving undergraduate research awards since the 1930s, and the National Science Foundation, which hosted a conference on undergraduate research in 1953, and the Research Corporation, which gave an undergraduate research grant to Pacific Lutheran College in 1959. But none of those had the impact of UROP. UROP was started by a physics professor and visionary dean, Margaret MacVicar. Though MacVicar died young, at age forty-seven, in 1991, the program she developed became the model for undergraduate research in the United States and the world.

The basic idea was simple. The institution would broker the interaction between a set of eager, talented undergraduates — most of whom did not know how to approach professors — and professors who wanted to add undergraduates to their research teams of graduate students

---

1 https://libraries.mit.edu/mithistory/institute/offices/undergraduate-research-opportunities-program-urop/

and postdoctoral fellows. The effort educated both groups about the possibility of collaboration.

At the time, and even more so today, graduate students who are barely older than undergraduates are carefully selected for PhD programs, in good part on the basis of their research potential. But this is not true of undergraduates. Therefore, interested faculty members have the logistical problem of attracting undergraduates with talent and maturity, of setting expectations for what they will do, and so on.

When I started using undergraduates on my research teams, most of my colleagues and I used our classes to recruit students who were serious. We also relied on word of mouth from our current undergraduate or graduate students. I remember seeing for the first time in 1986 a large UROP pamphlet that listed the names of the MIT faculty, the nature of their research, and how to contact them. It seemed so simple to just write it all down. By then, MacVicar had won over MIT's faculty and had established a robust program. UROP at MIT remains so today, and has expanded to include faculty fellowships, awards, and other activities.

Perhaps not to be outdone, Caltech began the Summer Undergraduate Research Fellowship program in 1979. It was started by Fred Shari, a natural scientist and chemical engineering professor, with eighteen students and seventeen mentors. The program has grown now to over 400 students and 200 mentors in an intensive ten-week summer program, and reaches outside of Caltech to attract students from around the world. Many other institutions have established programs to include undergraduates in research, often using the title, UROP. The University of Michigan, for example, began its UROP in 1988 with 14 students and 14 faculty members and now has over 1,300 students and 800 faculty members.

The universities have found these programs to be a selling point, in recruiting new faculty as well as students. Described in their admissions recruiting materials, the programs attest to both the excellence of their faculty's scholarship and their accessibility to students. In recruiting students, UROP-type programs give outstanding students a direct connection to advanced and prestigious academic work and mentoring from experts in specific fields, which top students crave. Students believe that such programs will give them an advantage in applying to medical, law, business, and other advanced degree programs—and they are right.

By now, it is big business in universities to offer undergraduate research opportunities. One of the best recent applications of this thinking I have seen is the Co-op Scholars program that is applied to freshman at the University of Massachusetts at Lowell.[2] Here incoming freshman students are given small scholarships to work with faculty in research to get them started right away in this practice and effectively counter the notion that undergraduate research is only for upperclassmen with some classroom experience under their belts.

Role of Departments

The other end of the spectrum of scale from the university is the academic department. Given that they are the focus of a particular area of scholarship and teaching in a university, they are a natural place in which to organize undergraduate research opportunities. The question is how does one get them interested.

Sometimes departments have even backed into such programs almost by accident. For example, I chaired the psychology department at Northeastern University for a few years in the mid 1990s, and before that served as the undergraduate head advisor. That department had a commitment to teaching undergraduate laboratory courses on topics in psychology ranging from perception to personality, and from behavioral neuroscience to cognitive psychology. The teaching laboratory classes were small, generally taught by professors, held in the department's own teaching

---

2 https://www.uml.edu/BeyondU/coops/Co-op-Scholars/co-op-scholars.aspx

laboratory space, and required a graduate teaching assistant — all of which meant they were expensive to run. As the number of psychology majors grew, those courses became a challenge to put on in sufficient numbers to meet the student demand.

The department also had an independent study course on the books that permitted undergraduate research with a faculty member in their research laboratory, provided that students could find a faculty member to accept them. The department faculty agreed to allow one of these independent study courses to substitute for one of the required teaching laboratory courses, perhaps as much for expediency reasons as well as for academic reasons, and the results were phenomenal. Prior to that point, my memory is that the department had perhaps 10 undergraduates per year taking independent study, but that number quickly grew to about 100 students a year after the change. The department could handle the capacity, given that it had about twenty-five faculty members with active research labs. I personally had about six undergraduates a year doing independent study courses in my research laboratory.

One of the issues that emerged was how the undergraduates approached the faculty to ask for the opportunity to do an independent study course (Blog Footnote 10.1).[3] It was not like signing up for a course on the registrar's system and showing up for the first day of class. The students had to talk to the faculty members.

Like the UROP program discussed above, the psychology department at Northeastern advertised the program to its students, but word of mouth was probably more important, particularly given the natural anxieties many students have about talking to faculty members outside of class. The honors program also helped. Students in the program typically

---

3 Blog footnote 10.1 *Undergraduate research - introduction achieved. Now what?* by Ashley Pira NU'12 and Jim Stellar, posted on 1/16/10 (http://otherlobe.com/undergraduate-research-introduction-achieved-now-what/). Also see the previous post from 3/25/09 cited in the opening sentence. These two posts show the anxiety of the first encounter but the eagerness for a mentor and how the concern was overcome despite contrary advice from an advisor that she was too early in her college career. Then in the second post cited above, one can see how it turned out after only a year when the student was seen as a regular member of the professor's laboratory.

did an undergraduate thesis with a faculty member and thus got to know them, often publishing a scientific paper together as part of the effort. These students could then introduce their friends to the concept and to the faculty member. Finally, the annual departmental poster day also helped. Here, senior-year honors undergraduates and others doing this research displayed their work in poster format. Students from all class years, even freshman, came to see what was happening and, in the process, witnessed firsthand the research relationship that had developed between the undergraduate and the faculty member.

The experience of working on my faculty research projects helped undergraduates from my laboratory, get into good medical and graduate schools or get jobs at biotech or other related companies in Boston. Word of those successes traveled, making our laboratory popular; students began clamoring to work there.

Undergraduate researchers also helped bridge the generation gap between the students and faculty and build a positive environment throughout the department. When I became chairperson, I appreciated how my own laboratory students provided me with an informal but rich channel of feedback on the academic and advising programs we were delivering. They made me into a smarter department chair.

By the time I became dean of the College of Arts and Sciences a few years later, many of our academic departments had adopted similar undergraduate research activities. The college, and later the university, began to hold expo days, were both undergraduates and graduate students presented their research. It was clear that undergraduate research opportunities were having a big impact on student success (Blog Footnote 10.2),[4] particularly when combined with cooperative education experiences where the students worked in industry or as paid research assistants with faculty.

---

4   Blog footnote 10.2. *Math, Molecules, and Woman*, by Rimma Pivovarov NU '10 and Jim Stellar, posted 1/23/10 (http://otherlobe.com/math-molecules-and-woman/). Rimma went from Northeastern University to Columbia University in a PhD program. She writes in the blog of a journey of self-discovery in that is typical of such students who used cooperative education to explore research possibilities. Her success in PhD program admission was made much more likely by this kind of personal growth and experience in college that went beyond just working in a faculty members laboratory.

Today, undergraduate research has become quite strong in many institutions and they typically highlight these opportunities to entice prospective students to join their institutions. Even small colleges have UROPs or something similar. Many institutions build research into their curricula or provide small stipends to students who take part. Some programs require it for graduation, such as the honors undergraduate major in neuroscience at Queens College CUNY, where I moved in 2009 to become provost.

Council on Undergraduate Research

The Council on Undergraduate Research[5] is the premier national organization promoting undergraduate research. CUR started in 1978 with a directory listing of undergraduate opportunities in chemistry in elite small colleges. The group held its first meeting a year later, electing a president; it launched a newsletter the following year. CUR held its first national conference in 1985 at Colgate University. Two years later it sponsored a conference on undergraduate research in Asheville, North Carolina, where in 1991 they opened a headquarters office. Along the way, CUR added other natural sciences and formed relationships with key federal organizations, including the National Science Foundation, which funds much of the basic research in the United States. Within the decade, CUR had become a national advocate for undergraduate research; it became a national organization and moved its headquarters to Washington, D.C. It also expanded its scope to cover all fields supported by the National Science Foundation. Other fields of research were added in the past decade or so, including the social sciences and the arts and humanities. Today, CUR has a membership surpassing 600 schools and 10,000 individual faculty members.

One aspect of CUR that I especially appreciate is its encouragement

---

5 www.cur.org

of faculty to be active researchers, even while they employ undergraduate research as a powerful form of teaching. That emphasis overcomes what I see as a false dichotomy between basic research in a discipline and teaching undergraduates. Professors generally become professors because they fall in love with their field. I certainly did. From the outset, they want to study it as well as teach it. Only later in one's career does competition develop between these two important activities, whether due to time pressure or other demands of a busy professorial life.

Scholarly Organizations

Another broad form of support for undergraduate research comes from the academic societies in specific fields. These professional groups hold conferences on their specialty. These meetings can be wonderful opportunities for undergraduates who are involved in research in that field, especially if the rest of their research or scholarly team—professors and senior researchers alike—is attending. A meeting with this kind of specialized focus kindles a more intense energy in undergraduates, compared to a conference or university expo at which many fields are represented.

Many scholarly societies now have undergraduate components that encourage research and attending the conference. My own Society of Neuroscience has a program called FUN, or Faculty for Undergraduate Neuroscience. It began in 1991 at a Society for Neuroscience meeting. Another regional organization in the area where I was a professor is called NEURON, for Northeast Under/graduate Research on Neuroscience, which was founded in 1988, and moved around between universities in the northeast region of the United States. The slash in the title indicates that the group encourages both undergraduate and graduate students to present their research. Other fields have similar types of programs and organizations, though the sciences have generally been in the vanguard of the trend.

The Society for Neuroscience's annual conference draws some 30,000 people from throughout the field of neuroscience. It's a massive show, so it was very useful for my laboratory to attend with many undergraduates and graduate students alike. Just like the graduate students, the undergraduates would fan out through the many simultaneous scientific poster presentations or talks, looking for interesting findings or techniques that we could use in our own research. We would each text the group when we found something of interest and that alone really helped me get the most out of a busy conference.

After the conference, on our return to the laboratory, the undergraduates helped us to reconstruct what happened. They loved being included. The biggest impact on them, however, typically came from their presenting their own work. Each year, I would have a poster presentation, or several of them, with undergraduates as co-authors, based on our work over the previous ten or eleven months. The student and I would start out together, in what typically was a four-hour poster session, explaining our work to anyone who walked up to us. Those browsers might be professors, graduate students, technicians, or other undergraduates. They might be from any university in the world. Often they were researchers whose scientific papers we had actually read. After an hour, once I had seen that my student was comfortable and capable explaining that piece of research, I would go and get coffee—not only because I love coffee, but also to leave the student in charge for a while. Sure enough, most of the time when I came back, the undergraduate would be engaged in good conversations explaining our research, often to professors, sometimes to my friends.

My favorite moments were times when an undergraduate breathlessly would tell me that a professor "just came up and was really interested in our work, saying it was related to his own research." The student would discuss the work with enough ease that the professor would assume she was a graduate student. That scenario took place more than once; on several occasions, professors offered students postdoctoral fellowships in their labs after the student completed her PhD degree with me. Of course, such an offer necessitated an explanation that the student was an undergraduate, not a graduate student. Observing the professor's stunned reaction, the student would appear to grow two inches. They were so proud of themselves and I was proud of them, too. More importantly, the experience of presenting the poster carried over to enhanced motivation to succeed back in the lab and at the university broadly. I have never seen undergraduates work as hard or be more passionate about research as when they return from such a conference. Undergraduates can be held back by the belief that they are not really ready to contribute to science, but this kind of conference experience breaks that restraint.

I am aware that attending a conference in the field of the professor costs money and it can be limited to those undergraduates who work with faculty who have major research grants. The college or university can help with travel grants as can the scholarly society. However, often such grants go to graduate students, not undergraduates. Nevertheless, the point still stands about the impact on undergraduate students of attending these meetings.

The Art of Teaming

A laboratory is like a family (Blog Footnote 10.3)[6] and when that kind of team dynamic develops, it can be very helpful to the laboratory leader and very powerful to the students. For example, for years, I ran a large neuroscience laboratory group that, at its peak, had three graduate students, a research professor, a technician, and about ten undergraduates, who were supervised by the senior people. The entire group met weekly, devoting about half of the time to lab operations, such as ordering supplies or maintaining

---

6 Blog footnote 10.3 *Undergraduate research: A lab as a family enhances the experience* by Lauren Donohoe, and others, posted on 7/2/10 (http://otherlobe.com/undergraduate-research-a-lab-as-a-family-enhances-the-experience/). This post describes what it is like to work in a lab as a group under a professor who cares. It is the largest number of authors of any blog post, which may say something. A key word in the beginning of their story is "teamwork."

the machines, and the other half on presenting our recent experimental results or reading relevant research papers from other laboratories. Undergraduates took part in every facet of the group's activities, and that created a dynamic whereby everyone knew one another and all about our work. I was pleased that the more experienced undergraduates helped the newer ones progress.

In this organization, I gave myself the responsibility of teaching each undergraduate the key principal techniques needed for the laboratory to operate. That helped me to keep our techniques consistent and to judge whether a student had the ability to progress toward getting his or her own project. Since we often took in freshmen or sophomores, that developmental process could take years.

I thought the system was working well, but when I became dean of the College of Arts and Sciences, my time in the laboratory had to be reduced. I had to let my experienced graduate students and senior undergraduates do more of the training. I had to monitor from a distance rather than teach each step.

Two things happened immediately. The first result was that the laboratory became more productive! It turns out that my insistence upon teaching the key techniques was a bottleneck; once I had released the grip that I had inadvertently imposed, my experienced colleagues got to teach more. The second result was that by having a greater teaching role, the senior students were happier. Who knew? This was my group. I cared deeply about their experience, but I had overlooked this unintended consequence.

Nonscientific Undergraduate Research

So far, my discussion of lab experiences has catered to scientist-professors, like me. But as a college administrator, I have also worked to build up undergraduate research outside of the natural sciences, especially where it involves groups of students working together on a project. It is easy to visualize undergraduate research in the natural sciences—the student is assigned a spot at the lab bench and given a simple task, such as washing glassware, to get started. The involvement escalates from there.

The laboratory model for undergraduate research may apply as easily to some of the social sciences, particularly where they involve research techniques, such as administering surveys or doing statistics that can be taught to undergraduates and where the results can be shared. Conducting interviews and creating surveys may be the social science equivalents of working with a lab bench. Applying statistics to analyze data may be analogous to washing glassware. I have seen sociology students hold meetings with professors that were akin to laboratory meetings and even refer to themselves as being in a sociology laboratory.

When the research subject is in some areas of the arts and humanities fields such as philosophy or art, the analogies to laboratory research in the natural sciences become more strained. If the faculty member is writing a book on a topic in history or English literature, for example, it may at first seem hard to imagine how an undergraduate could make a useful contribution. In these fields, I have seen that undergraduates can do library research, develop annotated bibliographies, fact-check, chase down leads for new information, and work in archives. If they cannot be listed as an author on the work, then perhaps they could be given credit in a footnote. As in a laboratory group, where senior undergraduates teach younger students key techniques, humanities students can help integrate their peers into the professor's group. The same family dynamic can develop around the shared experience of doing work with a professor or a gradate student.

The performing arts are a special case in the arts and humanities area. I see theatrical productions led by professors as developing similar group work to that which occurs in a science laboratory; and the public performance of a play seems like presenting at a research conference. Given the emotional content of productions, the hope that the work will have impact, and the individual public roles that must be performed, there may be no better academic team on campus.

As a dean at Northeastern University, I found that theatrical productions made important contributions to general education in all majors where they could be in the productions; I often had discussions with faculty members comparing the academic maturation effect of theater and other performing arts to our other forms of experiential education. A professorial colleague, Nancy Kindelan, put this thinking about the special contributions of theater into a book, *Artistic Literacy: Theatre Studies and a Contemporary Liberal Education.*[7]

Conclusions

In undergraduate research, as with internships and other forms of experiential education, it is important to provide students with an authentic experience and with substantial time on task. Some undergraduates may just want a taste of research; whereas others seem ready to join their faculty member at a higher level and to become almost like graduate students, often staying with them for years. Like other forms of experience, the more time the student spends engaged in a high-quality research experience, the better. The same is true for a faculty member. In my lab, once the students had done lab work for several years and had a scientific conference under their belt, they were more like masters-level graduate students than undergraduates. They could think about the literature in terms of what they had done with their hands. They invented experiments, techniques, and even concepts. I published papers with them and watched them grow.

---

7 Nancy Kindelan, *Artistic Literacy: Theatre Studies and a Contemporary Liberal Education*, Palgrave Macmillan (2012)

CHAPTER 11:

Combination Forms of Experiential Education

The forms of experiential education that I have laid out in previous chapters are not the only options. For one thing, these forms can be combined, such as a study abroad with an internship abroad. But a combination may have more to it than meets the eye. Consider a class doing community-based research. It combines undergraduate research and service-learning, but it also delivers impressive benefits that employers seek in leaning how to work in teams while doing and presenting the research. Community-based research deserves more attention from higher education than it has received in the past.

Let us briefly discuss a few of these combination forms of experiential education and see where they can lead our thinking.

Study Abroad Plus Co-op Abroad

As suggested previously, study abroad combined with a cooperative-education work term abroad is a classic recipe. A student goes to another country for a term of classroom study, and then stays for another term to work in a business, agency, or other organization. In the co-op or internship, the student can deepen language and cultural competency as well as learn about the enterprise. I mentioned previously, in the chapter on study abroad in Blog Footnote 9.4, an example that resulted in the student's capacity to do well with "French on the phone," a skill that did not emerge strongly in the first term of study abroad but developed in a second term of co-op abroad, where that activity was required at the workplace.

At the other end of the spectrum is a whole program of study abroad between two universities that can result in two degrees and a serious combination of work, study, and global experience. Consider the bachelor of science degree in international business administration (BSIB) that is awarded by institutions that are members of a global network called the International Partnership of Business Schools (IPBS).[1] IPBS recognizes that many aspects of business education today should be global, just like so many of the companies that will employ their students.

Freshmen in the BSIB program at, for example, North Carolina State University's Poole College of Management begin college as you would expect. They take introductory business courses and foreign language study on the main campus. But then they add a full-time paid internship at a local company. And at the end of two years, the students go abroad to study business in the classroom of another IPBS school, such as Germany's Reutlingen University. Those students also work in their second paid internship in that country. When they graduate, they get two degrees, one from each institution. More important, they emerge with work-relevant fluency in both the language and culture of a country other than their own.

---

1 http://www.ipbsedu.com

Fluency in that second language and culture is a big deal, and few students can hope to gain it without such a program. Once done, the student is set up in a world of many languages to be involved in global activities.

Some years ago, when I was still a dean at Northeastern, I attended a conference on making liberal education effective with Richard Freeland, Northeastern's president at the time. There, an executive from a Fortune 50 company stated that she had found that new college graduates—even of elite liberal arts colleges—were smart and well educated but unprepared for jobs with her company overseas. The company she represented had to "season them" in domestic employment for a few years first. But she had found one group of students to be an exception and ready to go upon graduation; she pointed to my president. The students were graduates of the BSIB program at Northeastern University, which is similar to the one at NC State. They were ready on day one.

Community-based Research

I started this chapter by suggesting that this particular combined form of experiential education can have a uniquely powerful impact on students. One of its features is that typically the research is done as a class. Having a class format is gives the experience a standard academic structure, which makes it easy to understand and to fit into the budget of the university. The professor is assigned to teach the class as part of their regular teaching load. Even if the class requires a bit of extra financial support to help students visit the community research site, it is typically much less than, say, a chemistry lab would require.

But the class is not typical. Rather then a series of lectures and exams, the professor often prepares in advance some consultancy plan with a non-profit charity of service organization or even a local governmental agency that has a need for research on its operation. In other cases, the professor helps the students to find those community sites. In all cases that outside agency ends up requesting an analysis, a position paper, or other help on an issue of concern. The students then set out to satisfy that need the way any consulting company would. They work in teams under the leadership of the professor and to come up with helpful findings, analysis, and even plans for action.

It is not by accident that many community-based research projects have a real-world social justice component, which may be part of their appeal. The students work in regular class sessions but typically also do research and writing in teams outside of class, before delivering a report to the client agency. Ideally, they present their reports in person in the client's conference room, as though they were professionals at a consulting firm.

When students are taken seriously and treated respectfully, they usually go all out. When I was a dean at Northeastern in Boston, I traveled to a conference in Princeton, New Jersey, with a professorial colleague and his student assistant. I had seen students who were inspired by my colleague's course put in many hours of time and effort. At the conference, a professor from Florida told a story about one of his students, who devoted the equivalent of a full-time job on her class project, so much that it worried him. But she maintained top grades in all of her courses, and she was there at the conference and able to attest to the fact that the experience was the best one of her undergraduate career. To me, it seemed that the professor's strong mentoring presence was an important part of her commitment, but the student was also energized by the social-justice mission of her research project, which involved a diverse population in her own state that had been denied full community services. The student was convinced that her research was going to do something good for society.

It is important to point out that the student project may not be taken seriously by the outside agency if the professor is not closely involved, providing expertise and assurance that the research is valuable. Without that piece, the project may fall short of being a substantial experience for the student and the company, and may become just another classroom project exercise.

Capstone Courses and Virtual Projects

The same dynamic occurs in a senior capstone course in engineering or in business, where the problem to be solved is a real one that comes from industry via the professor or the school. This arrangement is typical in engineering programs. In the final project, an industry representative is often present to hear the final project. One can see the impact on the students in either case, as they arrive dressed uncharacteristically in business attire to make the final presentation. The impact can be real, making the experiences more authentic. Sometimes students are even hired by the companies who have gotten to know them in these capstone projects.

A recent example of such an industry-based project done within a classroom format occurred in the fall of 2015 at my current university, the University at Albany. Here we ran a course where three teams of eight students did a project in the business college called "Cybersecurity: The Threat from Within." Much like a capstone project, students used cases of past cybersecurity breeches and worked up an analysis of what happened, but they did so under the guidance of a virtual mentor from major industries who met with the students in teams through a software platform provided by a new company, iQ4.[2] Through this platform they could interact, do research develop responses, work with both the industry leader and one of the university's faculty members to develop presentations on cybersecurity case studies and how to avoid such breeches in the future.

Like many capstone projects, we did the presentation in front of the industry mentors even though we had to travel to New York City from Albany, New York, to make the presentations—a fact that may have enhanced

2 http://www.iq4.com/home.php

the seriousness of the experience. I sat in and it was a powerful experience for the students and the mentors, as well as for me, to see how professional the students were. Some students said to me that they were so inspired that they put as much time into this course as they did into all of the rest of their courses that term combined.

Service Abroad

It is interesting in that a few years ago it was really enough for an American college or university to form a partnership with another university or a commercial outfit, often called a third-party vendor, and send students to take classes abroad. Some students may have performed service on their own while abroad and the host university typically had some programs for their own students of which the American students could take advantage. Now that is changing. Students even at the time of college application ask about opportunities to do service abroad. Maybe it is due to the growing use of social media where Twitter can provide citizen-based updates from events occurring around the world, even when the governments do not want it. We all remember the Arab Spring phenomenon that in Egypt really took off with the aid of Facebook and other forms of social media. I have seen examples of NGOs or national service organizations, reaching out directly to college students to get them to volunteer their time while they have it when they are in college. A special target is what is called alternative spring break, but the service work can happen over the summer or other break periods where students can get away.

Colleges and universities are getting on the same page as these outside organizations in presenting their own programs of alternative spring break. They have an advantage in that such activities can take place as part of a spring-term course, where the students sometimes even fundraise to support the trip that is seen as a field experience inside the course structure. Beyond spring break, universities are finding service opportunities for students on study abroad and including it as part of the total abroad experience. Industry is responding to develop programs and is starting to connect with the study-abroad offices.

I see the service abroad trend spreading to foundations and other funders. On my previous campus at Queens College, I saw the abroad office exploring a foundation-funded scholarship program, where the donor organization now not only wanted to support study abroad, but also wants to add a service component. It is an additional burden for the higher education institution to arrange and monitor service abroad experiences along with study experiences, but it is also an additional opportunity for deeper experiential education in what can be a very powerful setting. I see the same thing happening at my current place, the University at Albany, with our new efforts to enhance international experiences.

As an aside, it is important to note that educational institutions from high school to college have been running domestic service trips for years. Churches have also been running them for quite some time. These experiences can powerfully take students outside their comfort zone by transporting them to places where they have never been. We saw this effect even domestically, after Hurricane Katrina flooded New Orleans in 2005 or more recently when Hurricane Sandy flooded parts of New York and New Jersey in 2012. These trips can have many of the same elements of team building, mentoring, and personal growth offered by trips to foreign countries. But to my mind, there is still a deeper impact when the student does service in another country, language, and culture.

Winter-Term Field Experience

The winter term, for those colleges or universities that have it, is typically about a month long. Often this term is lightly used for regular course work, giving the winter term a feel on some campuses of a partial vacation period. To my mind, this is wasted time that colleges could better use by offering many types of experiential education, which would nonetheless give those students a break from the academic course routine. Some smaller colleges have been doing a winter-term field placement for years;[3] larger universities are beginning to catch on.

These winter-term field experiences can occur on or around the campus with no need for substantial travel. Some students may do community service in the neighborhood while others take part in business-plan competitions using open seminar rooms to meet and work out their final presentations. Students can do full-time undergraduate research in the laboratory or library to give a lift to the part-time work done when classes are in session in the fall or spring terms. The winter term can have a good back-effect on the rest of the academic year, as projects done in the fall can allow students to begin to master some of the skills needed for those business plan competitions. Examples here include a fall-term virtual project course or the year-long commitment to undergraduate entrepreneurship, as will be mentioned below.

At the end of winter term, students can be organized to make presentations about their projects, which can allow them to see each other's work and help reinforce their reflection. We started to do some of this winter-term field programming when I was at Queens College, but we never got to the cross-fertilization that is possible with a winter term Expo or some other conference event where the various activities are brought together. Thus, we also did not see the general benefit to the campus in enhancing experiential education in general.

Model United Nations and Other Simulations

So far, we have focused on direct activities rather than simulations, but they, too, belong to a class of experiential activities that can be very

---

3 http://www.bennington.edu/academics/FieldWorkTerm

powerful. The model United Nations is a simulation of an important international activity. It goes back to the 1920s and the League of Nations that predated the United Nations.[4] There are many ways for a student to participate in Model UN activities in putting together on-campus teams and making off-campus trips to Model UN conventions.

At its essence, Model UN has groups of students representing various countries; within each delegation, each student represents an individual or office. Students often do a great deal of research, debate current topics, learn about themselves and their teammates, and travel together to a convention. The performance is typically judged, which gives students feedback on their performance, based on knowledge and quality of presentations. Since it is a team activity, the Model UN allows students to practice an important job-related skill of working in teams toward a common purpose. While local competitions do exist, the students often travel, which introduces them to new places and often requires that they learn how to raise funds to help pay for the trip.

A fundamental value of the program for U.S. students, in my opinion, is that it gets them to look at the world from the perspective of another country. In this way, the Model UN has a small resemblance to study-abroad programs.

There are many other simulation experiences, including the debate team, math competitions, Robotics First, and so on. Some of them are long-standing traditions that are widespread, well organized, and provide participants with robust experiences every year. As a higher education enterprise, we could probably make better use of such simulations. The advantages are practical, as the simulations can often begin in the institution and may end there. Moot court in a law schools is one example, especially with the outside judges to add an element of the real world to what is an internal activity. In a previous chapter, I criticized moot court as being less

---

4 http://www.unausa.org/global-classrooms-model-un/how-to-participate/getting-started/frequently-asked-questions#how_did http://www.nmun.org

authentic and substantial than a law clinic, at which a student interacts with real clients under appropriate supervision, but that does not mean moot court is unimportant. It is a powerful and standard simulation of outside, real-world activity.

Simulations are used to great effect in industries or situations where it is too costly or dangerous to go to the real-world situation. Consider the flight simulator for the training of pilots, which today provides a very realistic experience and allows student pilots to make mistakes without causing damage or loss of life. But notice that a flight simulator is a highly refined technology, which does not come cheap. When one is in it, the simulator seems real, even though everyone knows it is not. Of course, with ever-increasing computer power, simulations grow ever more sophisticated and realistic, so this is an important future area in higher education even at the undergraduate level.

Business Plan Development

In some respects, development of a business plan is a kind of simulation. Many business schools at universities offer business-plan exercises and competitions for their students. Students divide up into teams and solve problems with prizes often going to the best solutions. The competitions can occur in many places in the curriculum, including the winter-term field experience, as mentioned above, or at other times at the end of at term, or even within an individual business school class.

In each case, there is typically some outside involvement from alumni or local business leaders that lend the activity some gravitas. And unlike other simulations, a business-plan development exercise can actually lead to the formation of a business, sometimes with the students getting jobs out of it. When students make that jump, the college can then celebrate them in public relations and recruitment materials as successful entrepreneurs, which has an encouraging effect on other students. By bringing together students and businesspeople, business-plan development can also lead to internships and experiences that promote student development.

Entrepreneurship

Entrepreneurial activities are everywhere on campuses these days. They come in the form of student clubs; individual, professor-led activities; whole programs that are often within business school; and broad-based institutional activities like the Blackstone LaunchPad,[5] where the goal is to infuse the entire campus, well beyond the business school, with entrepreneurial activity. In the fall of 2015, my institution, the University at Albany, won one of five new Blackstone LaunchPad grants for universities in the state of New York, and is now, at the time of this writing, fully engaged in making a successful launch of the program.

Some students thrive in this environment and even start real businesses, ranging from products and services, to cell phone apps and other online activities that leverage the modern Internet and social media world. Not all have to be companies like Facebook or Twitter to have the potential for real-world application that draws in the time and energy of students. Without leaving the campus, the students and their professors can undertake an activity that can provide a very powerful substantial and authentic experience.

CUNY Service Corps

Many institutions provide scholarship or fellowship funds to support students doing service thus combining part-time paid internships with service. The Service Corps of the City University of New York (CUNY), discussed already in Chapter 8, does that. To review briefly, it is a fairly new program that deserves mention again due to its impressive

---

5 http://blackstonelaunchpad.org

scale. Launched in the 2013–2014 year, CUNY's program paid over 700 students annually to work from twelve to fifteen hours weekly for twenty-four weeks. Supporting that payroll costs millions of dollars, not to mention the expense of a new administrative structure to oversee the placement and oversight of students, their interaction with the provider, and the payment process.

Future assessments will examine whether the experience that continued the following year will increase student retention rates, further the students' use of internships, and develop their overall success in college and afterward. But already, as a member of one of the campuses that won a chance to have its students take part, I have seen a positive impact on my previous institution's other service programs in the first year and more broadly on experiential education. In short, it has developed student leaders, drawn charitable organizations to campus, increased the engagement of the campus with the outside world, and provided other such benefits that come from making porous the walls of the so-called ivory tower.

Theatre

A theatrical production is an interesting way to turn classical academics into an experiential activity right on campus. Theatre goes well beyond courses on public speaking, because it draws in students' emotions and can interact powerfully with their unconscious decision-making process. In general, creative expression performed before an audience—whether in the visual arts, dance, or poetry reading exercises those hidden decision-making circuits, as highlighted in David Eagleman's 2011 book, *Incognito: The Secret Lives of the Brain*.

That fact that a college theatrical production is seen by an actual audience, even if generally from the campus community, makes a big impression on students. Theatre is also a team activity that usually requires participating students to invest a great deal of time and effort. Note that the same can be said for sports teams, which suggests that sports may offer similar opportunities to teach team-based leadership. Theater programs have even been claimed to help develop an institution's general education efforts, and a book was written on this topic, interestingly from a professor at a cooperative education school.[6]

Student Leadership

Discussions about leadership often start by listing positions of authority in student government or clubs. But students can experience leadership in many other ways, such as on teams where leadership roles shift as the event unfolds. In exercising leadership, students gain benefits of experiential education, when they use unconscious decision skills to navigate social situations, read other people's nonverbal cues, or put themselves in others' place and imagine their reactions. I will address leadership more directly in Chapter 13.

Working on Campus at a Paid Internship

Many student jobs on campus can promote student growth while helping the institution. Campus writing centers, for example, are perfect places to employ students; they give invaluable help to other students who need a bit of help, especially those for whom English is a second language. To be a writing center tutor is to have a job, so maybe we should not even consider it an internship. But with just a little work to build in some academic oversight and reflection, that job, or others like it, can have more of an impact on the student who holds it than one might expect.[7]

Universities benefit from employing students, too, and I'm not just talking about enthusiastic work for relatively cheap. Student employees can

6 Nancy Kindelan, *Artistic Literacy: Theatre Studies and a Contemporary Liberal Education*, Palgrave Macmillan, 2012
7 Blog footnote 11.1 *Learning while tutoring in writing*, by Chloe' Skye Weiser, QC '13 and Jim Stellar, posted on 12/5/12 (http://otherlobe.com/learning-while-tutoring-in-writing/). The writing center brings in the international student among other types. In this blog, the Chloé describes what it was like to learn to think outside her perspective to help this student, what it was like to be a mentor, and how that related to other experiences she had such as a trip abroad.

also add a level of insight and credibility to the operation, especially if it is directed at other students. Several years ago, students working in my office tipped me off, for example, that Twitter was surpassing Facebook as the favorite form of social media on campus, and that I should not rely on Facebook alone to advertise campus programs. I might not have picked that up as soon on my own.

Finally, if the institution believes in experiential education, how can it not make the most of opportunities within its own business structure to employ students, and at a fair wage? How could we ask companies to do what we ourselves would not do?

Experiential Education Is Now Everywhere

We could continue with more forms of experiential learning that are not what we defined in the previous chapters as standard forms. Some of them will be combinations of the standard forms. Some of them will seem more unique. Some of them will be readily accepted and others may cause one to pause and think about whether that is so. All of this discussion is good, as long as a fundamental principle of experiential education is at work, distinguishing it from traditional academic education. In my view, the fundamental principle is, first, that the activity has an impact on the student's unconscious processes, which can change through learning and experience; and second, that it fits with or otherwise informs the student's career choice by complementing the academic learning about a subject.

This principle is at its most productive when the experiences complement and reinforce the academic learning, although alumni have repeatedly told me that some of their best decisions after completing an internship or some other college experience were to leave a field to enter a different one. In my personal history, I realized that I would be happier in a research laboratory than in medical practice. To this day, I am grateful to the professor who challenged my thinking and directed me to the experience I needed, working in a research laboratory, to test my interest.

Someday we may be able to run an fMRI or other type of brain scan on a student and determine the impact of an experience on what field is most suited to that person. Frankly, I hope not. I think there never will be a substitute for young people inventing their own futures. But whatever future they choose should be based on experiences that reveal how they process information and operate in various fields, and how much they enjoy them. Let's keep the student in charge, while we in higher education doing everything we can to help them figure it out.

CHAPTER 12:

The Value of Reflection

For a typical college student, reflecting on experience seems like a waste of time. The experience is what matters. To educators, reflecting on the experience is what draws out the learning. Only by reflection can a student integrate an experience into thinking, say, about a choice of major or the area of employment to pursue after graduation.

So what is reflection and how do we get students to do it in higher education? A reflection component of an experience could be anything from a group conversation to a graded paper or something else entirely. Naturally, adding a reflection component to an experience demands extra time and effort of both students and faculty. But time and time again, we see that investment in reflection is powerful (Blog Footnote 12.1),[1] and will

---

1 Blog Footnote 12.1 *The power of reflection – a story from Greece* by Adrienne Dooley and Jim Stellar, posted on 11/24/12 (http://otherlobe.com/the-power-of-reflection-—a-story-from-greece/). While staffing a study abroad experience in Greece, Adrienne had a powerful encounter with a student doing a final report on her project. The student had an insight into the "privileged life" she had led as a member of the majority culture in America vs. the life she might have had as part of a minority underclass. This kind of reflection, which is best done within a group that has established a positive social dynamic, can help the student perceive new things about herself.

pay real dividends in terms of student learning.

As discussed throughout the book, I think brain science has something to say about reflection, and that is found in the strong evocation of the instinctive mental process of unconscious decision-making by the experience itself. A proper experiential activity, as mentioned repeatedly, is both substantial and authentic; therefore it is also immersive. It captures what Daniel Kahneman[2] calls the "type I process" that is fast, always on, and operates unconsciously. It is through this kind of learning, that I believe the student becomes familiar with the workplace and its tasks, and develops the beginning of expert knowledge that contributes to their observed maturity when they return to campus. That instinctive process, of course, complements the more rational, mental process we see in the classroom, which we use to teach facts and theories that will also be operating in the experiential activity. I believe reflection connects the instinctive process to the rational, and it is especially needed if the experience is very intense or fast-paced, allowing little time and rational mental space to reflect while it is happening.

Interestingly, forming groups can be very important to triggering a rich reflection on experience. A reason groups are important derives from the evolution of the human brain during the last 40,000 years or so, when humans lived mostly in small groups. Those groups helped humans survive, enabling them to pass genes to the next generation. According to this concept, known as the social brain hypothesis, the brain at this late stage in the history of our species, evolved to promote effective group dynamics that shape our behavior today. With apologies to social psychologists, I'll introduce this concept by discussing three amazing brain facts that could facilitate human social interactions today, and therefore enhance experiential learning through reflection. Each brain fact should inspire more research. Some of these brain facts were previously mentioned.

---

2 Again the reference is Daniel Kahneman, Thinking Fast and Slow, Farrar, Straus, and Giroux, New York, NY, 2011

von Economo Neurons

The first brain fact is simple. Inside the brain are large, spindle shaped, highly interconnected neurons that appear to exist only in primates and a few other highly social animals. Humans have more of these neurons than any other primate. To a neuroscientist, any type of neuron that is found in unusual numbers in humans and our closest cousins, but not in other mammals, is inherently interesting. A set of neurons that are so highly interconnected with other neurons is even more interesting. What do these neurons do? Some neuroscientists think they may be responsible for the conscious awareness of unconscious processing of emotions. I believe that they may also be seen as supporting the function of reflection on experiential education (Blog Footnote 12.2).[3]

To give a bit of history again, these neurons are named von Economo neurons after their discoverer, Constantin Freiherr von Economo, whose career spanned the first third of the twentieth century and overlapped with the first neuroscientists to study the fine anatomy of the neuron shape. Two of the most famous neuroscientists from that period are, Santiago Ramón y Cajal and Korbinian Brodmann. Respectively, they used a method developed by Camillo Golgi, whom Cajal shared the Nobel Prize with in 1906[4]. They stained then characterized the basic microscopic appearance of individual nerve cells. They showed how to use that cellular structure to divide the large cerebral cortex into discrete brain areas, which were later seen to underlie discrete behavioral functions such as vision.

What von Economo found was neurons in the insular cortex and the anterior cingulate cortex, two cortical areas that were discussed in Chapter 6 as being key to unconscious decision making. The von Economo neuron's cell bodies are large in size, permitting very long processes that can connect to many other neurons in many brain regions. To use an outdated

---

3   Blog footnote 12.2 *The Insular Cortex, von Economo neurons, and awareness of feelings*, by Ilyssa Monda-Loiacono, Golshan Aghanori QC'13, Jungyo Kim QC'13, and Jim Stellar, posted on 9/13/13 (http://otherlobe.com/the-insular-cortex-von-economo-neurons-and-awareness-of-feelings/). This blog post, based on the laboratory work of Professor John Altman, looks at the insula cortex and von Economo neurons, which may play a role in shaping feelings that underlie the process of reflection, and which allows facts-and-theories" conscious thinking to be guided by our unconscious decision making processes
4   https://faculty.washington.edu/chudler/nobel.html

analogy, these neurons are the brain's telephone switchboard operators, or perhaps the computer routers of today.

It is likely not a coincidence that von Economo neurons tend to be found in brain regions where emotional properties of pleasure and pain are socially integrated with higher cognitive functioning. One example is the anterior insula cortex, which fMRI shows to be activated when a person watches another person who is in pain. The watcher "feels their pain" in these brain areas, in a cognitive, if not a sensory, fashion. Neuroscientist Antonio Damasio contends that this kind of integration, which occurs in various places in the brain, is part of what produces consciousness. He identifies the insula and anterior cingulate cortex as examples of these convergence-divergence brain zones in his book *Self Comes to Mind*.[5]

Jonathan Haidt, a researcher on morality and ethical leadership at New York University, makes an interesting analogy on how we make decisions consciously versus unconsciously to the hypothetical choosing of the direction in which an elephant-rider pair is leaning or going.[6] In the analogy, the decisions are made on the basis of size with elephant representing the unconscious process. The conscious speaking part of the brain is then like the small human rider who is left to use words to explain why it is a good idea to go in that direction.

How might we use our mammalian brains and perhaps our von Economo neurons to make experiential education better? I think you already know. We must pay attention to the unconscious conclusions of the mammalian brain in higher education, even if the conscious brain does not recognize where those feelings come from but takes them as its own. We do that by setting up good experiences and then by having reflection as part of the process to help connect these two brain functions. But before going further into this topic, let us explore a second, amazing brain fact.

---

5 Damasio, Antonio. *Self Comes to Mind: Constructing the Conscious Brain*, Vintage Books, New York, NY 2012. Note: For the present discussion, I am sidestepping the important issue of the nature of consciousness so we can stay focused on how the results of the unconscious decision processes of the mammalian brain transfer to a person's conscious decision making primate brain; but see the book *Incognito* by David Eagleman.
6 Haidt, Jonathan. *The Righteous Mind: Why Good People Are Divided by Politics and Religion*, Vintage Books, New York, NY 2012.

The Cerebral Cortex and Its Neurons

The second brain fact concerns the cerebral neocortex itself, the crowning achievement of brain evolution that ended in a massive enlargement in the brains of mammals, and particularly humans and other primates, and that gave humans high-end cognitive abilities, including language.[7] Because it is the most recent big step in brain evolution, as mentioned in Chapter 4, we call it the *neo-* or *new* cortex. What concerns us here is the surprising discovery by British anthropologist Robin Dunbar that the size of the neocortex correlates well with the size of the social groups in which humans and other primates typically live[8]. The group size for humans is between 150 and 200 people, the typical size of a primitive tribe, or the number of "friends" with whom people actually regularly interact on Facebook or Twitter. Now many species have what is called a Dunbar number. It makes sense that, if the neocortex underlies our computations of how individual members contribute to a group's functioning, we would need a bigger cortex to keep track of a bigger social group. If bigger groups are more effective in producing evolutionary benefits, then one can see how this connection to bigger brains could develop.

The connections between nerve cells in the neocortex (and beyond) form a network. Networks are fascinating and are an even newer area of neuroscience as well as in many other fields from social science to computer science. Networks are said to have *emergent properties*. Phenomena or processes can occur in a network that cannot be observed in any of the individual units that comprise the network. You need the individual units to be together to see the emergent property. In fact, you may not be able to learn much about such emergent network properties by studying units as individuals.

An example of an emergent property can be seen in the traffic patterns of a network of roads and motorized vehicles. One cannot really understand traffic merely by studying the construction or driving properties

---

7 For a sophisticated account of neocortex evolution see either http://www.ncbi.nlm.nih.gov/pmc/articles/PMC3973910/ or http://www.ncbi.nlm.nih.gov/pmc/articles/PMC2913577/
8 http://www.psy.ox.ac.uk/team/robin-dunbar

of a car. To understand traffic, you must to get the car on the road with other cars and a host of other factors, such as weather, breakdowns, and road construction. Mob mentality in human interaction is another phenomenon that requires the individual people but only emerges when you have a group of people interacting as a network.

Let's assume that the basic network function of the cerebral cortex is indeed established by evolution, in part through the social evolutionary influences described above. Are there any other factors that could shape it in our lifetime? One of the ways networks operate is to prune back connections that are not used. This happens early in live as initial experiences shape the basic structure of sensory areas. But it is easy to see how it could continue to shape and make efficient the networks underlying thinking at any level—conscious decision-making or unconscious-decision making. Since we continue to replicate the group living that our ancestors pioneered, there may be many ways, including using pruning, that the groups in which we live shape the very brains we carry into any situation, including going to college.

Oxytocin

The third brain fact is about the hormone oxytocin. This small protein is released in the body and causes feelings of affiliation. It has achieved some fame in lay society and some call it the "cuddle drug" or the "love drug," although it is neither a drug nor so simple in its function.

Oxytocin does two basic physiological things in the mammalian body. First, it is released by the pituitary gland during the birth process to produce the uterine contractions that lead the mother to deliver her child. Second, it is released by the pituitary gland during nursing to produce milk letdown in the breast. Oxytocin's release is triggered by the suckling of the infant at the breast, and thus it is part of a tactile-neuro-hormonal reflex that involves two individuals working together to accomplish the goal of feeding the baby. It is easy to see how, as humans evolved, oxytocin also could come to help mother and baby bond socially, which became more and more important as primate brains grew ever larger with evolution and took more time to develop. Humans, of the entire animal kingdom, require parental care for the longest period of time.

The surprise may be that oxytocin brain circuits also exist in men, who do not have labor contractions or nurse babies. To successfully carry their genes into the next generation through their offspring, men also had to play a role in caring for the infant. Having two parents turns out to be very helpful for raising a human. From that point, it is not hard to imagine how oxytocin could be adapted, through natural selection, to help produce bonding between fathers and their children and then between parents and even between adults in the group. That bonding turns out to be very important to the functioning of a group.

Today psychologists have studied oxytocin in many situations, in part because it can be safely administered as a nasal spray. They wanted to see whether it produced increased generosity within a group, and it appears to do just that. People receiving oxytocin treatments are, on average, more willing to share resources such as money within their group. It is said that the best natural way to produce high levels of oxytocin in the blood is to give someone a welcome hug-a reflection of existing social bonds and a way to produce even stronger connections. A phenomenon such as bonding has to be more complex than the action of a single protein, but it looks like oxytocin plays a role, even if is not a cuddle drug.

But again, there is a twist. It is well known that if one is in a defined out-group, and if an out-group is perceived as a threat to your in-group, oxytocin can have the effect of reducing generosity toward the out-group member (Blog Footnote 12.3).[9] Possibly the trick in leveraging oxytocin's

9 Blog footnote 12.3 *Taking Ex Ed into international relations*, by Lara Porter and Jim Stellar, posted on 4/23/12 (http://otherlobe.com/taking-ex-ed-into-international-relations/). Oxytocin produces more generosity in members of the in-group,

affiliation-producing properties, or any other mechanism of group cohesion, is to define the members of an out-group as really being part of a larger in-group before administering oxytocin. If all of humanity is defined as your in-group, then you would be smart to treat all humans with generosity.

We will return to this discussion of relations between group members in the next chapter. For now, the existence of these brain mechanisms, and many other facts of human psychology or neurobiology, suggest the power of groups in shaping our behavior, consciously or unconsciously. Perhaps that also extends to reflection.

The Need for Group Reflection

Now we can see why, as discussed in Chapter 9, some of the traditional study-abroad students who were asked to reflect individually by keeping a journal tied to specific calendar dates, instead made up their journal entries with minimal effort while on the airplane on the way home; whereas the students who were on the faculty-led trip could not stop reflecting at the end of every day. Students in the faculty-led trip had a strong group. The topics of reflection were from their shared experiences, and the problems they were trying to solve came out of that natural social interaction.

Even in my experience of doing science, practitioners learn much from one another. That is why doctoral programs in the sciences often involve years of working in the laboratory of a more senior scientist. In the four years I spent earning my PhD, I took courses for only about one and a half years; by that calculation I probably spent seventy percent of my time in graduate school in an experiential education mode as an apprentice to my advisor at the lab bench. I was doing science and publishing while being a

---

but in negotiations with another group, it could produce the opposite as members of the in-group rally against the out-group, particularly if there is a history of strife. In the blog post, Lara and I raise the issue of whether a study designed to increase perceived flexibility of mind in the other group, was really not a way of making us see the out-group as part of our larger in-group of humanity so that oxytocin and other social brain mechanisms would produce a better outcome.

junior member of a laboratory group and learning like crazy from everyone. Lab meetings were a chance for me to see if the ideas I had derived from reading and experiments would stand up to my intellectually powerful social group. The principles of science ruled, but the group helped me to learn. I was like the college students on the faculty-led trip abroad, but my trip was at the lab bench.

Unconscious Decision Making Revisited

Now that I am an administrator and no longer work in a laboratory, I sometimes have a hard time convincing students and faculty members of the value of reflection. In addition to the time required, there is another ancient reason why, which can be summed up in the adage: You don't know what you don't know. On the surface, that idea seems to be simply about information, but is about more than that. Today we know that many of the brain's processes happen outside consciousness and tend to defy verbal understanding (Blog Footnote 12.7).[10]

A person often does lack the information he or she needs—and does not know it. In fact, we may never know what is inside us and how we reached a specific decision. This idea, as previously expressed, begins with a unit of the brain that Michael Gazzaniga calls the interpreter module.[11] The interpreter module "talks" but the circuits that generate those words appear to have no direct access to the computational brain circuits that make the emotional, gut-level in what the book calls the mammalian brain. The interpreter module instead typically takes the unconscious mind's conclusions as its own, without actually examining them.

Gazzaniga illustrates that last point by describing an experiment we were all taught when I went to graduate school.[12] A surgeon has treated

10 Blog footnote 12.4 *Wisdom, unconscious decision-making, and experiential learning*, by Darya Rubenstein and Jim Stellar, posted on 12/22/14 (http://otherlobe.com/wisdom-unconscious-decision-making-and-experiential-learning/). This blog post explores the concept of wisdom as an unconscious mammalian brain process, based on an audio file posted by a Jewish rabbi discussing the Hebrew term *da'as* (deeper/intrinsic knowledge).
11 Gazzaniga, Michael, *Who's in Charge?: Free Will and the Science of the Brain*, HarperCollins, New York, NY, 2011.
12 This story is told in the Gazzaniga book mentioned above, but I have heard it many times.

a patient's intractable epilepsy by separating the left and the right cerebral hemispheres by cutting the biggest fiber bundle in the brain, the corpus callosum. The operation succeeded, and after recovery, the patient wound up in a psychology lab for testing.

In the experiment, the patient was seated in front of a tachistoscope, a machine that shows simple words or a picture to be flashed in one side of the visual field or another. The tachistoscope works because the patient looks at a fixation point between the two visual fields, left and right, and the machine flashes the images too quickly for the patient to move his or her eyes from one image to the other. Yet the machine does not present images so quickly that the patient cannot easily recognize them. Given the way the eyes connect to the brain (and here I leave you to look it up online if you want), the image presented to the right side of visual space is perceived only in the cortical hemisphere on the patient's left side of the brain; the image presented to the left side of visual space is perceived only in the right cortical hemisphere.

In most people, particularly in right-handed males, the left cortical hemisphere is the brain region from which spoken language originates. So, if you flash a picture of a ball on the right side of visual space, the patient is able easily to say the word "ball." If you flash a picture in the left visual field, perhaps of a key, the patient will say that he saw nothing. In a way, that's true, because the stimulus is now encoded only in the patient's right hemisphere and not the "speaking" left hemisphere due to the split-brain procedure. We know that the stimulus that is encoded in the right hemisphere is not lost, because the left hand, controlled by the right hemisphere, can reach into a hidden box under the table and unerringly pluck out a key from an assortment of small objects.

In the version of the experiment that interests us here, the tachistoscope presents the split-brain patient with two images at once—a ball is flashed in the right visual field at that same instant that a key is flashed in the left visual field. Under these circumstances, the patient naturally says, "ball" and the left hand naturally finds the key in the hidden box.

But now the fun begins. The patient is sitting in the chair looking at the left hand holding up the key for both hemispheres to see. When the left hemisphere sees the key in the left hand, it immediately makes up a story. The patient might say, for example, "You need a key to open the cabinet where the balls are kept." That is a potentially logical statement, but it is totally made up.

Because I am a professor who gave essay tests, I am aware that students sometimes make up answers when they do not know the relevant content, perhaps hoping they will say something that earns them partial credit. But they know they are doing this. This speaking split-brain patient does not appear to know. Of course, most people are not split-brained, and what is known in one hemisphere is transferred to the other. So, does this logic apply to most people? It does, but in a slightly different way.

Let me share another story. Many years ago, I had a distant relative who developed a malignant glioma, a brain tumor, in the right occipital lobe of his brain. This is the place in the neocortex that gets the input from the eyes. As a result, he became blind on the left side of his visual space in both eyes. My relative essentially could not see anything to the left of where he was directly looking. That disability stopped him from going for walks, because as he told me when he reached a street crossing, he would occasionally be surprised by a car that seemed to appear out of nowhere from his left side. Yet he never figured out that he could not see the left side of his visual space. I tried to explain to him this left-side blindness, and even suggested that if he looked left-right-left when he crossed a street it would be a good strategy; for when he turned to look left the second time, both sides of his visual field could see any cars. He did not take my advice, and frankly I did not press the point, as gliomas typically are fatal. He instead took his walks on the arm of someone else, which made him feel safe about crossing the street. But his very young daughter had figured out what was happening. She knew that if her dad was watching television, and if she was sitting on his left side, she could play with his deck of cards that he normally would not let her touch — as long as she did it quietly. Dad did not know what he did not know.

If the location of my relative's brain tumor had been a little different—for instance, so that he lost the input from the left visual fields from both eyes to his right visual cortical region—he would have known he was blind in the left side of visual space. He would have seen it and complained about it. The interpreter module would have known it. My relative likely would have adopted coping strategies such as the one I suggested. But if the injury is in the higher cortex region itself, the brain area that processes the input, the patient acts as though that part of the visual field does not exist, never existed, and there is nothing to worry about. It is a very interesting difference in the mental experience that results from changing where in the pathway the visual stimulus processing is interrupted.

How do such cases in which a person does not know what he does not know apply to experiential learning? Well, in similar fashion, we apparently do not know what we do not know through our unconscious decision making in the mammalian brain. Our interpreter module, does not keep track of where it got the information about why that major or this career path might best suit us as an individual person. Sometimes, we have to work, with reflection, to be able to consciously understand our own choices.

Meanwhile, the von Economo neurons, or some other brain mechanisms, apparently do make us aware of our unconscious decision-making, by processing our experiences through the 200 million-year-old emotional circuits perhaps in the limbic system. We get a feeling that a situation is good for us or not good, but then, focused on the interpreter module, we usually are unaware of the calculations behind those inputs or where the decision came from. Some people may have, or may develop, better awareness of or use of these sources of information from the limbic-system, mammalian-brain, unconscious decision-making brain circuits. Perhaps such people are better at making decisions. "Old souls," for example, are said to have wisdom and wisdom is said to come from experience. Again I refer you back to Blog Footnote 12.4.

In my opinion, our institutions of higher education have a huge blind spot when it comes to the workings of the mammalian brain. I think college and university courses and the curriculum those courses support almost exclusively address the interpreter module in our students. Then we release them after graduation into industry or more schooling to figure things out on their own using both processes. Throughout its venerable history, higher education has been fixated on facts and theories — in curricula, the course syllabi, certification of academic knowledge, and the awarding of degrees. Is it any wonder that higher education does not address the whole student, or that it devalues the mammalian brain processing that is adept at learning from experience, and may ultimately determine what a student decides should be their major field of study? In this regard, colleges and universities seem oblivious to Pascal's insight: "The heart has reasons of which reason does not know."

Social Brain Mechanisms of Reflection

I still have hopes that higher education can give reflection its due. As stated, evolutionary changes in our brains were spawned by the need for humans to work well in groups. And there is a way you can talk to, and learn from, your own mammalian brain by engaging with another person. While, I am a big fan of people solving intellectual problems in a group, here I mean something different. When someone talks to another person face-to-face, not on e-mail, they engage in a running nonverbal conversation that emerges from their mammalian brains, their unconscious decision-making processes, and it runs along with the verbal conversation. They may not be aware of this non-verbal conversation, but they are picking up slight changes in facial expression or body posture and those signals are typically processed unconsciously, rapidly, and effortlessly. That signal is what the other person thinks at gut level (Blog Footnote 12.5)[13]. This kind of reflection tends to surface and examine the unconscious decisions we are making ourselves in college.

As I mentioned, when I wanted to tell my mother that I was switching my career goal from medical school to graduate school, I rehearsed my story with my college roommates. I figured that my mother had wanted me to be an MD so much, that I had better prepare my speech. I knew the facts-and-theories content of what I wanted to say, but I wanted to know in advance how presenting it would feel. I wanted the experiential component to go with the knowledge component. I wanted my mammalian brain to help me present what I would say from my primate brain. Fortunately for me, when I did it, Mom was gracious.

For similar reasons, students should be talking to other students about what they learned from experience. Again as I described in Chapter 9, students did that naturally on the faculty-led trips, and students just as naturally and artfully dodged those conversations when we required them to submit individual timed journals that they wrote and backdated while in flight during their return to the United States.

That is why, in experiential learning, a good reflection component needs to engage students for more than a single assignment of a few hours. It is best if the communication activity is repeated. It is even better if it is concurrent with the experience. It is best if the activity is done face to face and among people who care about one another. I am not saying that

---

13 Blog footnote 12.5 *Nonverbal Communication and Experiential Education*, by Vanessa Castro and Jim Stellar, posted on 3/17/12 (http://otherlobe.com/nonverbal-communication-and-experiential-education/). In this blog post, we consider the power of nonverbal communication and even facial emotions in influencing a student who is having an experience such as a paid internship or any form of experiential education. The post urges a sensitivity to culture and to the need for active communication, which can be encouraged or discouraged, something that may be especially important to a minority culture in the workplace. We finish by discussing the engagement of attention, which is a classic mammalian brain idea.

classical academic work like a paper is bad. But I do think that the work has to produce conversation during its development or presentation, or both, and the more the better. Relying on the student to write a paper alone is not enough; such an activity denies the participation of the nonverbal mammalian brain component of group reflection that fires the gut-instinct and emotional brain circuits so that the student can evaluate and re-evaluate the experience, what it means, what the knowledge is really telling the whole student.

C H A P T E R   1 3 :

Social Capital, Tolerance, and Leadership

What is the primary function of a college education? Some think it is to broaden a young person's mind, building tolerance for different ideas and people. Such an education of the mind, by that view, seems necessary for effective citizenship, especially in a democracy composed of many different types of people. Others argue that the purpose of a college education is, first and foremost, to teach critical thinking in a recognized field, preparing the student to be productive in a career, either with or without further schooling. Some emphasize that college is a good place to teach responsibility, if the young person has not learned it already. No matter which function is regarded as most important, I think most would agree that all of those qualities are necessary for the molding of tomorrow's leaders.

But I see another function of college—one that appeals to me as a scientist and advocate of experiential education—that also provides a key to leadership: Teaching students how to build and apply "social capital" to promote growth in themselves and the people around them.

What is social capital? The term refers to the networks of relationships among people who live and work in a society. A person who is skilled in building and using relationship networks—the webs that enable society to function effectively—is sometimes called a social entrepreneur. My observation is that entrepreneurs of all stripes tend to become leaders.

Our world is growing increasingly interdependent as the populations across the globe, which have been separated for much of our human history, come to interact through travel, commerce, and even social media. As this happens, we need to graduate more students who are social entrepreneurs. We need them to help us as global society figures out how to interact productively. As some say, this is the problem of our time. That takes us to diversity. A common goal of many higher-education institutions is simply to successfully integrate students from all backgrounds to improve their learning for a modern global world. My own belief is that we must take the opportunity of diversity to educate the next generation of tolerant, critically thinking, socially entrepreneurial leaders. I think that experiential education offers unique ways to do that. Let's explore how.

Social Capital

The basic definition of social capital as society's networks of relationships is simple enough, but becomes more complex when one gets into it. While relationship networks are as old as humanity, the term social capital was used widely only after the late 1980s, when sociologists Pierre Bourdieu[1] and James Coleman[2] used it in their writing. Now it is commonly used.[3]

1 Bourdieu, P. (1986) The forms of capital. In J. Richardson (Ed.) *Handbook of Theory and Research for the Sociology of Education* (New York, Greenwood), 241-258.
2 James S. Coleman, *Social Capital in the Creation of Human Capital*, American Journal of Sociology 94 *Supplement* (1988): S95 – S119
3 http://www.socialcapitalresearch.com

We all know the saying about financial capital: "Money is power." Social capital is similarly a form of power among people. Social capital may be created by a personal relationship, such as friendship, or from the status of being a famous or admired person.

The World Bank's website discusses the concept: "A narrow view of social capital regards it as a set of horizontal associations between people, consisting of social networks and associated norms that have an effect on community productivity and well-being. Social networks can increase productivity by reducing the costs of doing business. Social capital facilitates coordination and cooperation."[4]

Social capital can also be vertical, transcending the group, at least according to the World Bank's discussion. Vertical social capital can produce even greater productivity for individuals by expanding the possibilities beyond that group and perhaps limiting some of the us-versus-them side effects that can come from strong identification solely within one group. Extending social capital in that way seems to touch the whole society, with its systems of politics and its legal adjudication, keeping people following a common set of rules and allowing them to be productive on a very large scale.

My point is that there is much to this concept of social capital, and many of the forms of experiential education — such as internships and service-learning — involve activities that generate it. As mentioned, my colleagues and I have written about this issue of social capital a good deal starting with a student who was at the time studying economics (Blog Footnote 13.1)[5] at Northeastern University and including one working in the Center for Ethnic, Religious, and Racial Understanding (CERRU)[6] at

---

4 http://icnie.org/2014/01/what-is-social-capital/
5 Blog footnote 13.1 *Social Capital and Experiential Education* by Carolina Morgan and Jim Stellar, posted on 10/18/13. (http://otherlobe.com/social-capital-and-experiential-education/). Beginning with the concept of social capital and its manifestations in classical situations of microloans to women, we look at its development through Carolina's own college and post-college experience leading to graduate school. We discuss how it can facilitate individual action, which in an experiential education college/university context comes across as enhanced student maturity and commitment.
6 Again http://cerru.org

Queens College, CUNY (Blog Footnote 13.2).[7] Such activities can have an impact on the education of individual students, enhancing their personal development, as the students find places and power in the social order of the professional fields they enter after graduation. We know that from the recent Gallup-Purdue poll on workplace engagement and what helped in college.[8]

Tolerance

Social capital can have many uses, as we plan for experiential education in higher education. As I mentioned earlier, some consider teaching tolerance an important function of higher education, and certainly social capital itself can produce tolerance, as I have seen occur in the CERRU program I just mentioned. In many public universities tolerance is needed due to the demographics of the student population but it is especially true at Queens College CUNY, where I had the privilege of being provost for four years, and which resides in perhaps the most diverse borough in the United States. At this institution, students typically come from more than 160 countries and speak more than 60 languages, with about 40 percent of the students born outside the United States. The CERRU program explicitly aims at training students to walk in each other's shoes without pushing participants to adopt the views or position of those from a different background. The goal is to understand and engage in dialogue respectfully, even if people disagree.

This state can be hard to reach, however, due to the social dynamics that identify certain groups as in, or popular, and others as out. This pushes such groups apart, especially if they are competing with one another, as indicated in by Jonathan Haidt.[9]

---

7 Blog footnote 13.2 *Social Capital and the Queens College Experience* by Lara Porter and Jim Stellar, posted on 1/17/13. (http://otherlobe.com/social-capital-and-the-queens-college-experience/) Beginning with three forms of social capital: bonding, bridging and linking. The blog discusses the application of bridging social capital in the Center for Ethnic, Racial, and Religious Understanding (CERRU.org) at Queens College CUNY to build relationships between groups that might ordinarily clash due to rivalry. While the ultimate goal might be to turn on what Jonathan Haidt refers to as the "hive switch" in his book *The Righteous Mind* to produce an in-group bonding experience the feasible goal is to achieve respect for, if not acceptance of, each other's positions.

8 http://www.luminafoundation.org/files/resources/galluppurdueindex-report-2014.pdf

9 Jonathan Haidt, *The Righteous Mind*, Vintage Books, New York, NY. 201

Joshua Greene, in his book *Moral Tribes*[10], makes a useful analogy between two forms of our moral reasoning: one between members of an in-group, and the other between members of two different groups or out-groups. He argues that the two forms of reasoning are like the two modes of taking pictures with a modern camera: automatic or manual. When we reason about folks within our group, we tend to use the automatic mode, which reaches rapid decisions using instinctive brain circuitry that is likely more involved with unconscious-decisions rather than the brain areas that make decisions more logically and to which we have greater conscious access. When we reason about members of out-groups, however, the automatic mode often gets the decision wrong, especially when those groups are in competition with our own group. To make the right decision, Greene argues, our automatic reasoning must be tempered by what he calls the manual mode—conscious, deliberative reasoning. We will return to this dual-mode of thinking, with further consideration of Haidt's formulation of how we operate. But this concept should not be strange to you, as it comes out of our previous discussions of the evolutionarily newer primate brain versus the older mammalian brain.

Self-mastery

Social capital can also refer to the development of the self in ways that can be applied in a social context, including the workplace, as opposed to the development of abstract skills or the mastery of academic facts and theories. Thus, social capital often gets mixed into the teaching of soft skills, such as behaving effectively in working groups, team leadership, communicating knowledge, and navigating issues of global diversity. But social capital is distinct from soft skills, being more about self-knowledge and even confidence.

The contribution of social capital to leadership is apparent in women's college sports, which has flourished on college campuses since

10 Joshua Greene, *Moral Tribes: Emotion, Reason, and the Gap Between Us and Them.* Penguin Press, New York, NY, 2013

passage of Title IX of the U.S. Education Act.[11] It is widely recognized that participation in competitive sports develops leadership (Blog Footnotes 13.3)[12] and other such skills that business require to function. Although we would argue that women and men may not make decisions in exactly the same way (Blog Footnote 13.4),[13] one way that a complete college education can produce women students who can take leadership positions within the business community is through sports (Blog Footnote 13.5).[14] Gender differences are a topic that deserves much more attention but goes beyond the scope of this book, so I will leave that discussion here.

Social capital concepts are seen in business too. Everyone knows that the bottom line typically refers to whether an enterprise makes money or not. In my lifetime, the *monetary* bottom line has been joined by the *green* or environmental bottom line. More recently, it has been joined by the *social* bottom line. The latter refers to the social good the company does with its operations and even its profits. Many people, for example, would like to do some good when they make a purchase, even if it means they pay a little more for the product-hence we have locally grown produce, free-range poultry and meats, and socially responsibly sourced coffee.

The public expects that non-profit organizations, including most colleges and universities, build social capital partly by striving for a higher standard of social good in their operations than in simple for-profit enterprises. We saw this outcome decades ago, when colleges joined the

---

11 http://www.justice.gov/crt/overview-title-ix-education-amendments-1972-20-usc-1681-et-seq

12 Blog footnote 13.3 *Freeing the Mind: Eradicating Gender Inequity in Higher Education with Experiential Learning and Insights from Neuroscience* by Naomi Ducat, posted on 7/7/14. (http://otherlobe.com/papers/freeing-the-mind-eradicating-gender-inequity-in-higher-education-with-experiential-learning-and-insights-from-neuroscience/) This short paper by a college student emphasizes the need for using higher education experiential techniques to teach leadership to underserved populations, particularly women.

13 Blog Footnote 13.4 *Women, Decision-Making, and Experiential Education* by Rachel Eager and Jim Stellar, posted on 8/15/15. (http://otherlobe.com/women-decision-making-and-experiential-education/) We cite two studies in this post that suggest that women have similar decision-making process to men. These data stand in contrast to Rachel's own experiences of microaggression and other forms of discrimination that still exist in the modern world and may relate to unconscious decision-making. Higher education and experiential education methods, in particular, are seen as having potential to contribute to leadership development in both women and men.

14 Blog footnote 13.5 *Women, Leadership, and Sports—Learning from Experience* by Cynthia Bainton, Kush Sidhu, and James Stellar, posted on 8/4/13. (http://otherlobe.com/women-leadership-and-sports-—-learning-from-experience/) Women in leadership positions as an adults appear more often to have played sports in their youth. This may be because they learn something there that helps them "lean into" their careers, as Sheryl Sandberg discusses in her 2013 book, *Lean In: Women, Work, and the Will to Lead.* This post examines that book and competitiveness concepts in a three-way conversation that draws on lessons from directing an urban ice hockey program for high school women in Washington DC.

campaign—some grudgingly—to divest in companies that had dealings with apartheid-era South Africa.

Today, social media creates social capital by building communities, often for profit. Interestingly, social media companies rely greatly on the voluntary contributions of individual members, which may move the social media phenomenon into social psychology or sociology. Still, social capital can be made and used in any place where humans interact, online or in the real world.

Intolerance and Tolerance

One of the most pernicious forms of intolerance stems from the in-group/out-group arrangements mentioned earlier. As the literature on the topic points out, the human ability to handle complex social problems within a group through cooperation may have evolved as part of the competition among groups for resources. The largely unconscious, intuitive decisions we make about members of our group are important to keep some people from taking advantage of the cooperation of others in the group, thus undermining the group's competitive ability in an evolutionary environment where other better-functioning groups would prevail.

Oxytocin, as discussed in Chapter 12, is known to enhance group cooperation within a group but also to enhance competition with other groups identified as outsiders. People are also very sensitive to indicators of group membership, even down to accents in speech and, of course, physical attributes. Even infants perceive a non-native speaker when they themselves are at the later stages of pre-word babbling within their own language.[15] The same intuitive logic that keeps us acting in way that is fair within our group—such as sharing resources with those who share with us—can easily turn into the punishment of group outsiders, by causing members to withhold needed resources from outsiders. That is why colleges with diverse

---

15 See Joshua Greene's book cited above for a more thorough discussion of this literature.

populations of students will always need tolerance-building programs. There will always be a tendency to see people who are outside our group as less deserving of our compassion or support. Of course, one way to get around this problem is for the whole university to clearly act as one group, and that typically happens when one university competes with another in, for example, a sporting event. At the game, it matters much less whether a classmate cheering for your team is from your ethnic group, class, or social organization.

Social capital has the potential to build tolerance for those who are not in our group, which in turn can generate more social capital—a virtuous cycle, where students succeed in a modern world composed of many ethnic, religious, and racial groups that come together in an unprecedented and important ways. The jobs most students will get after graduation will require teamwork with different types of people—and those differences are ever more likely to have a global nature. Any business today, even if it considers itself domestic, is increasingly affected by the global environment, making tolerance necessary for employability, if it is not sought for its own sake.

There are at least three basic ways that social capital operates that could foster tolerance, according to the literature in the fields of sociology, social psychology, and economics. First, there is instrumental support, which could be anything from expanded opportunities to learn new skills on the job, to a reference from the boss for a new job in another company. Students use their built-up, instrumental social capital when they ask a professor for a reference to apply to graduate school or professional school. I always urge my students to get to know a few professors in their college education, which is why undergraduate research or mentoring of students on a service project is so important in experiential education. It naturally develops those ties.

Second, building social capital helps in simple information gathering. Think about how we all like to get breaking news from a friend, and then how we, or at least young people, tend to look it up on social media. We want our students to have that kind of insider knowledge about their potential careers after college. Students should and do trade experiences about what happened on an internship.

Third, social capital provides psychological support, in the form of encouragement and even moral support. While an academic advisor may give a student information about classes and even may recommend a field of study, a mentor goes a step further and explains the value of that information and treats the student as if he, or she, were a close relative, perhaps recommending specific instructors where an advisor might not.

Not long ago, a former student of mine sent me a note that illustrates how social capital can create a virtuous cycle. He wrote the following, which I quote even though it is a bit long: "Everyone who has a relationship to anyone, a friendship, can immediately understand how these ideas work. And thinking about how careers get started, I can bet anyone who has gone through a cooperative education program can come up with an example of how someone at their first internship—a boss, a colleague—helped them in some way get to the next step in their career. For me it was bosses (and deans!) who loved to mentor and recommended me to get into great grad schools. They also advised me on career paths and which experiences and classes to seek to make me a better professional. They gave me tips on how to write my essay and CV, and they pushed me to go for the top schools even when I doubted myself. Peers and colleagues were also an invaluable source of information about our discipline and the possibilities out there for young professionals. This is how social capital worked for me. In turn, I began to advise our new interns at work who intend on following in my steps and adopt my approach of learning and openness to what others have to say."

My former student's comment underscores the role of mentoring in the generation of social capital. It is noteworthy that the student himself became a mentor to others. An old saying about teaching, "You never learn something so well as when you teach it," also applies to mentoring. But, even more than traditional teaching, mentoring networks create social capital.

What we need to do in higher education is to extend those mentoring networks from the classroom to the places where our students work or learn as part of their experiential education. Imagine how universities might harness the power of social capital in these mentoring networks when their professors are connected to their students in the external experiential education world. I have seen this phenomenon occur when I was at a cooperative education institution.

Leadership

So much has been written about leadership that I hesitate to try to add anything. But leadership is one of those qualities that we expect universities to bring out in their students. And leadership is an essential complement to social capital, tolerance, and experiential education. And of course, society needs leaders of all types, from the citizen-leaders who contribute to their communities and teams without much recognition, to the more obvious hero-leaders who are out front and everyone knows it.

Experiential education can do much to strengthen leadership skills, especially by exercising students' unconscious decision function, which combines with a strong intellectual function to make a good leader good. Having great ideas is not enough; a leader has to convince other people to implement them (Blog Footnote 13.6).[16] Excellence in both types of function need not occur in the same person, but when they do, that individual possesses real power to lead. We all have seen the charismatic

---

16 Blog Footnote 13.6 *Leadership Uses the Other Lobe of the Brain Too* by Cynthia Bainton and Jim Stellar, posted 5/18/09. (http://otherlobe.com/leadership-uses-the-other-lobe-of-the-brain-too/) Some leaders seem to know how to lead people. In this blog post, we explore one such case from the commander of a U.S. Navy destroyer who delivered high performance, under budget, with attention to the sailors at all levels who served on his ship. We see applications here to learning from experience on top of an excellent academic college curriculum

type of leader who does not have a firm grasp of content. When a leader, by contrast, has both charisma and command of content, he or she can move the group ahead. Author Jim Collins emphasized those two aspects in his famous book *From Good to Great Why Some Companies Make the Leap...and Others Don't.*[17]

Another important facet of leadership is strategy. In a 2007 book that I understand is popular among business leaders, William Duggan analyzes the careers of two influential military strategists: Antoine-Henri Jomini and Carl von Clausewitz.[18] According to Duggan, Jomini developed the kind of strategic planning that starts with a goal and then maps a clear plan to get there. The Jomini method is highly logistical, managerial, comprehensive, and can be rationally detailed.

By contrast, von Clausewitz pioneered a kind of strategic planning that incorporates intuition — or what I am calling unconscious decision-making processes — along with logic and analysis. In this method, intuition often comes in a flash that brings with it both the goal and the strategy to get there. Duggan contends that Napoleon Bonaparte, one of history's most famous military leaders, planned his many brilliant military campaigns using the von Clausewitz form of strategy. My point is that unconscious decision processes can be a very successful contributor to leadership.

If higher education is about producing future leaders and entrepreneurs, we may be short-changing our students by overemphasizing the Jomini kind of strategy. In the facts-and-theories classroom, we do not really teach the von Clausewitz kind of strategic thinking. We should, at the very least, have students exercise those brain circuits, through a good dose of experiential education (Blog Footnote 13.7)[19].

---

17 Collins, James, *Why Some Companies Make the Leap...and Others Don't*, Harper Collins, New York, NY, 2001
18 Duggan, William. *Strategic Intuition*, Columbia University Press, New York, NY, 2007.
19 Blog footnote 13.7 *Does* Entrepreneurship *come from Experiential Learning?* by Allyson Savin and Jim Stellar, posted on 5/10/10. (http://otherlobe.com/does-leadership-come-from-%C2%ADexperiential-learning/) This blog post focuses on entrepreneurship where a kind of fluid free-form thinking is characteristic of success. The post also calls to mind the unconscious decision-making circuits that lead to strategic intuition of other forms of intuition that are essential for these activities and may be taught best by hands-on experiential education programs.

Let me underscore that I am not denigrating classroom instruction. A leader needs command of the facts and theories. Napoleon, as Duggan points out, was very well schooled. But a leader also needs the intuition and judgment from the unconscious decision process, an area that the classroom is poorly suited to teaching. Universities should be looking to experiential educational to supplement standard classroom-based programs and teach leadership and entrepreneurship. Once again, this idea is not new, but with our improved understanding of the brain, perhaps it is time to embrace it fully.

Our Inner Elephants

I want to return to Jonathan Haidt's analogy of two types of thought to the relationship between an elephant and its rider.[20] The rider, or conscious thought in this analogy, is astride the massive elephant that represents the brain's unconscious function of decision-making. If the elephant really wants to go in one direction, it simply does so. Meanwhile, the rider, as he is being carried away, as stated, becomes the equivalent of a press secretary who explains why he wanted to go in that direction in the first place. The rider might not even be aware of the factors that chose the direction. As David Eagleman suggests in his book *Incognito*, we typically are not aware of our unconscious influences; we think that the conscious "I" made the decision when sometimes it is our more intuitive process that is setting the direction.

Haidt's analogy is also powerful in discussing how two political adversaries as riders may have difficulty reaching agreement. As discussed, he describes a scene in which two conscious, decision-making riders are mounted on two unconscious decision-making elephants, one elephant leaning left and the other leaning right. The riders may not even see each other and their rational arguments can literally talk past each other. Sound familiar in today's politics? To encourage the elephants to begin to "lean"

20 Haidt, Jonathan. *The Righteous Mind*, Vintage Books, New York, NY. 2012

in each other's direction, Haidt recommends that one leader may pay an innocuous compliment to another perhaps on an item of apparel. That may get them to lean toward one another, just a little. While such a gesture may not transform the dialogue by itself, it might start building social capital between adversaries that could lead to conscious decisions to look for common ground.

We discussed the conscious versus unconscious decision-making processes in the previous chapter in connection to the concept of the social brain. Now we are applying it here in terms of social capital. Because the brain, especially the unconscious brain, is powerfully affected by non-verbal cues, and because those cues provide a running commentary on the content people exchange through conscious thought, it matters that people have some positive experiences with one another, even starting with an small compliment on something innocuous.

It is true that we may observe a frown and know consciously that the other person disapproves of our statements. But it is also true that we may not be aware of why we have a feeling that things are going well or not well in a job interview or in a work situation. We are likely unaware of the release of oxytocin in a social situation that causes bonding and maybe increases our prospects at turning an interview into a hire. But we have to be able to negotiate that environment of social interaction in almost anything we do. Experiential education offers opportunities to practice, learn, and generally figure out how that level of thought works and to do so in a field that we intend to enter.

Remember my mother's comment when I was on my first internship, and turning from medicine to neuroscience research. She said she'd never seen me so excited about anything except surfing. When she said that, I felt it was true; it crystallized something in me. Of course, no individual had more social capital with me at that time than my mother.

Principles and
Practices of
Experiential Education
Implementation

CHAPTER 14:

Institutional Principles and Experiential Education

Now that we have discussed how experiential education works at the level of students (and their brains), let's consider briefly how colleges and universities might operate at the level of the institution. Then in the next chapter, we will do the same thing for practices. We are getting a bit away from the student focus of this book, but given the institutional need and the appreciation I have for that given my long service in administration, I cannot resist making a few points. If this topic does not appeal to you, skip to the afterword. But do read that before you close this book.

I also have to say that this chapter is not meant to be an exhaustive survey of institutional principles, but rather a general look at what are operational principles in the first place. I am mindful that many people have studied how universities work as professors as part of their research.

Not me. As you know, I am a professor of neuroscience. I do recognize the expertise of these colleagues in higher education the same way I would like my own professorial expertise to be recognized. So, I will approach this discussion of principles from my experience as an experiential education practitioner and as a university administrator. I hope it gets you reading some of the many works published in this field, a few of which appear in the footnote below[1], and others of which have been cited throughout the book in the text and other footnotes.

The General Principle of Emergent Property

Neuroscientists like looking at systems on at least two levels at the same time. For example, in the brain we study the ways nerve cells work together to form neural circuits and how those circuits then add up to behavior. We say that the behavior is an emergent property of the brain in action, just like traffic emerges from the cars in action on our roadways, as already mentioned.

In the same way, I see the university as composed of its faculty, students, and staff who group together to form programs and departments and colleges that, in turn, add up to the essence of the university. You may see that essence in the general reputation of a university or at specific times like at graduation where the university spirit or energy or pride is on display. That display is an emergent property - all those people and programs in action over time produces the hopefully happy students at graduation. While we not only produce the educated graduates who know their stuff and can think critically, we also have actively helped the student develop a path to what comes next, be it the job they want after graduation or admission to graduate school for further study. This is one of the emergent properties that I want to see more of in higher-education institutions.

---

1 For example: Asia-Pacific Journal of Cooperative Education http://www.apjce.org, International Handbook for Cooperative and Work-Integrated Education http://www.waceinc.org/handbook.html,

Certification of Knowledge in the Course through the Credit Hour

As our first institutional principle let's consider how colleges and universities collectively fulfill one of their most fundamental tasks - to judge what knowledge its students have gained so that we all know what goes into a college degree. One way we in higher education do this task is by using the ubiquitous credit hour. Credit hours are as fundamental to college as roads are to our daily travel life; like roads, they define much about how we go about our business, but we hardly ever think about them. They are just there. In a way, they are a hidden principle, but hidden in plain sight.

Ironically, the credit hour first came into widespread use when the Carnegie Foundation used it in the early 1900s as a tool to help determine professors' retirement pensions.[2] Today, retirement for professors is largely handled by pension programs that have nothing to do with the credit hour. Since then, it has persisted as a useful organizing device to define the time a student spends in a course. It is considered a rough measure of the knowledge gained in that course, despite the concerns, including those of the Carnegie Foundation, that we need more modern measures of learning.

By this system, a three-credit course is worth more than a two-credit course, both in class meeting time and in potential knowledge gained. When the faculty of a college or university approve a new course, a thorough debate typically occurs about whether the proposed course fits within the standard framework of expectation, including the number of credit hours earned. Approval of new courses and maintenance of academic standards and accreditation are key parts of the academic management of the degree content—and all are pinned, in large part, to the credit hour.

Consider, for example, "Introduction to Chemistry," a three-credit course that has an accompanying one-credit laboratory section. The student earns four credits for the entire package. The course consists mostly of lecture, which along with reading has long been considered the

---

2 https://www.luminafoundation.org/files/resources/carnegie-unit-report.pdf

most rapid and efficient delivery system for facts-and-theories knowledge. That component is three hours a week for three credits. The laboratory, by contrast, meets two hours a week but is worth just one credit—or half the rate of credits per class hour of the lecture component.

Why is the laboratory part of the course worth less? Having taken, taught, and overseen many laboratory courses, I can tell you that the difference is based on the implicit assumption by the faculty members like me that lab-based learning takes place at a slower rate, largely because the students do the work themselves. To mix chemicals in test tubes takes time. Sometimes it does not go well and must be repeated to achieve the result required for the laboratory report on which the grade is based.

Many forces today are challenging this assumption of needing separate parts of such a course. I will venture a guess that the increasing adoption of online courses with online laboratory-type exercises may make obsolete the division between lecture and laboratory sections. In another innovation within the university, the so-called "flipped classroom," students view some or all of the lecture material online before the class period. That leaves the classroom for more active learning through group discussion and other techniques. In fact, when I taught my first three-credit flipped class in the fall of 2014 (Blog Footnote 14.1),[3] my experience was that there seemed to be many active-learning parallels to experiential educational activities.

The point here is that the credit hour provides a framework for certifying knowledge delivery in a course. If experiential education activities fit into the course, they are also certified under this credit-hour rubric, but if not, they lack this certification. When I was at Northeastern University, a leading cooperative education school, credits for cooperative education experiences were listed on the transcript. The so-called "co-op credits" did

---

3 Blog Footnote 14.1 *Bringing experiential education techniques to the "flipped classroom," undergraduate-professor partnership, and student engagement*, by Agata Buras and Jim Stellar, posted on 7/3/15 (http://otherlobe.com/papers/bringing-experiential-education-techniques-to-the-flipped-classroom-undergraduate-professor-partnership-and-student-engagement/) In this post we describe our experiences with an introductory psychology course which we offered in the basic flipped course framework with the idea of exploring the parallels with experiential education outside the classroom. From casual observation, those parallels are substantial and produce a powerful student engagement as revealed through in-class surveys and student reports. The discussion begins where a previous post by Shalini Singh left off, as mentioned in the introductory paragraph.

not count toward graduation, but they were an important placeholder on the transcript to show what students were doing when they were working full-time and not taking courses. I think we can and must do better in higher education going forward. What do I mean by that?

Certification of Knowledge in the Program through the Credit Hour

If a college bachelor's degree requires 120 credits and the average course is worth three credits, a student must take and pass an average of five three-credit courses a semester to graduate in four years or eight semesters. Universities keep a close watch on their students' progress, not only to help them stay on track, but also because the graduation rate is often used to compare the quality of a university. If a student delays choosing a major, fails a few courses, or somehow has not completed enough credits by a specified term, an advisor or faculty member may be alerted to intervene to help the student restore progress toward the degree. Increasingly, universities are using software and what is called big-data analytics to detect when a student falls off track in credit-hour accumulation or in other ways. The upside of what seems like a technical tracking is that students often appreciate the timely conversation with a university official helping them solve problems with their plan of study.

Colleges break down the total required credits or equivalent courses into categories that include the major, the general education or core curriculum, and electives. Students may add a second major or a minor, or even two minors; and such overachievers often graduate with more than the required minimum number of credits. To me, a little inefficiency in earning credits to graduate is worthwhile if the student can afford it and if the student is happy doing what he or she wants. Otherwise it might be better to graduate with only one major or one less minor and pursue the other interest in graduate school or in a specialized program after some time spent working. In the sciences, we often see students who decide late in their undergraduate careers to apply to medical school. Typically, they return to college after graduating to pick up the courses they still need. Such post-baccalaureate programs also exist for other fields.

As stated in Chapter 1, I know something about changing focus, in my case, on the basis of an internship at the end of my junior year. Fortunately, I stayed on track with my credit accumulation to graduation as a biology major. But that was just lucky, as I knew for the first time what I wanted from my college major program for my career. Someday universities may be judged not on how effectively we graduate students on time with 120 credits, but through big-data bases that show whether our graduates get the jobs and/or get into the graduate schools they want. Already, I see signs of this happening.

Finally, I have to also mention that the credit hour is important for those who are paying the tuition bills. In some places, students or their parents pay by the credit hour; but even if they pay by the term, colleges and universities set credit-hour limits on how many courses a student can take in a semester. If a student takes less than a certain amount, such as nine or ten credits, then that student may be considered part-time. Typically, schools that charge by the term allow students to take extra credits beyond the standard fifteen before levying additional charges. Such a rule allows a student to take one or two four-credit courses (e.g. a chemistry course with a laboratory section) as part of a full load of five courses a term, again without incurring extra charges.

Applying Credit-Hour Logic to Experiential Education Activities

But how does the credit-hour logic apply to learning from experience? Institutions typically do not award academic credit hours for experience activities themselves. As already mentioned, when I was there, Northeastern University did put cooperative-education credits on its transcripts but they did not contribute to graduation like academic credits. Johnson & Wales University, did give academic credit for learning associated with an internship but assigned a faculty member to oversee the related academic work. So the credit was not really for the experience itself, but for the associated academic work.

I like this approach. When I was a professor in charge of a behavioral neuroscience research laboratory, I ran many independent study courses for academic credit. I always required that each undergraduate student produce an academic paper with scientific literature references in the same style that was required for a standard course. But I also considered the length and form of the paper in light of the lab work the student did with his or her own hands at the laboratory bench. I usually asked the students to write a first paper in scientific format, with introduction, methods, and preliminary results, but I left off a detailed results section and a conclusion section for any second independent-study course.

For the methods section of that paper, the student wrote about the work that he or she had been assigned to do at the lab bench with their hands. To be clear, the experimental protocols done in the neuroscience lab were not the student's ideas. They were determined by whatever grant supported the experimental work, and they were approved by the university oversight committee that regulated research often from protocols we had submitted before the student arrived in the lab. Yet I felt through writing about the protocols and experimental procedures the students were doing, the students gained a deeper understanding of the entire research process. Thus, the assignment blended real-world learning from the laboratory bench with the academic learning of the classroom. And my students really earned their credit hours.

Does this approach work only in a laboratory? I think not. Not long ago, at Queens College, I supervised, with another faculty member, an independent study for a young woman who was pursuing majors in both art and economics. The student had arranged an unpaid internship with an art auction house. We asked her to keep a daily journal of her work experiences and to write a paper that was a reflective analysis of those experiences, although it also incorporated academic references and scholarly discussion. The paper was shorter than I would have assigned in an independent study without an internship; nonetheless, the assignment prodded her to glean academic learning from the experience. Incidentally, the task also helped keep the university and the company in compliance with the Fair Labor Standards Act,[4] in part because she elected to work there without pay.

Experiential Education and the Transcript

While we are making progress in bringing experiential education activities into the course structure, I find that universities often resist even discussing it outside that structure. They tend to call these activities "extracurricular," as though they were separate from the student's learning in college. This inherent conservatism was brought home to me in a 2011 talk I heard John C. Cavanaugh give in Philadelphia at the Middle States Association of Colleges and Schools conference on accreditation. He made an intriguing comparison between the ancient monastery and the modern university[5] that I find worth repeating.

Cavanaugh said that in the sixteenth century in England the elite controlled access to the Christian bible, which largely resided in hand-copied forms within the monasteries. The monks and members of the powerful elite doled out knowledge of the bible's contents to ordinary people through sermons and other teaching, not unlike traditional lectures in higher education. After the Gutenberg press began producing printed copies, the very first bibles were chained to the altar, and ordinary citizens were forbidden to have a copy of the sacred text, an offense punishable by

4 http://www.dol.gov/whd/regs/compliance/whdfs71.htm
5 Published in *InsideHigherEd.com* on 12/14/11 (https://www.insidehighered.com/views/2011/12/14/cavanaugh-essay-how-accreditation-must-change-era-open-resources)

death. Of course, that did not last long and soon copies of the bible were widespread in the land.

Cavanaugh then made an analogy between the text in the bible and the content of the college transcript. He referred to the transcript as the sacred text of higher education today, with the university being like the monastery, and faculty members as the monks. He worried that higher-education institutions today are holding onto the power of the college transcript, organized by credit hours, as the only valid means of certifying knowledge. Universities are reluctant to admit other forms of student learning that do not fit into the framework of the transcript and its credit-hour listings. Cavanaugh charged his listeners to think more deeply about how to measure knowledge gained in experiences outside the classroom. He urged us to deconstruct the degree process and get at what students actually learned.

You won't be surprised that I took seriously Cavanaugh's challenge to think. I could see, for example, that medical schools had long required students to complete a medical internship and residency before they could practice. That experiential component was required. Back in the 1970s, when I was a graduate student, the first part of medical school education was almost entirely classroom-based and the last part was practice-based in rotations in the hospital. My father, then a medical-school professor, often talked about how the required skills of the classroom and the rotations were complementary but different, and he noted how many of his students underwent dramatic reversals in their class ranking when they switched from the classroom to the hospital rotations.

Let's keep going with this medical school example. Medical students must learn various skills, such as recognizing medical signs that are more exacting than many skills students must learn in other fields. When Lloyd Jacobs, a surgeon and the then-president of the University of Ohio, Toledo, described his own medical education in a 2013 speech to the World

Association of Cooperative Education, he made a telling observation. He said that when an experienced surgeon first showed him a human body open on the operating table, everything looked the same; it was all pink and homogeneous. With time, he began to see what the surgeon saw. He labeled this awareness as a kind of visual learning that was not taught in the classroom but only through direct experience.

Jacobs asked the conference attendees to study that form of learning. I completely agree and am pleased to see that such research is increasingly taking place, resulting in papers published and presented at conferences around the world. For too long, learning from direct experience has been assumed to focus on soft skills that involve interpersonal interaction, the student's sense of self, and a primer for the workplace. But it is much more than that. I believe these experiences train the brain circuits associated with the mammalian brain, the unconscious decision process. When Jacobs, as a medical student, saw what the human body looked like on the inside, he was matching his developing visual and perhaps motor-skill knowledge with his conscious knowledge from the book learning of the first years of his medical training. He had started engaging both the primate and the mammalian parts of his brain.

To probe that idea a bit further, an undergraduate student-with whom I had written several blogs on another topic[6]-and I examined the accreditation requirements[7] for internships in a master's-level program in her speech language pathology department. We found that becoming a certified practitioner in this field required four items: a master's degree from an accredited program; passing of a professional exam; having an accumulated 400 hours of a supervised practicum; and working in a clinic, hospital, or private practice, followed by an additional 36 weeks of supervised clinical experience, called a clinical fellowship year. Note that two of the four requirements for accreditation are experiential.

---

6 See Blog Footnote 7.3 (http://otherlobe.com/internship-vs-undergraduate-research—what-is-the-difference/)
7 Accredited by the Council on Academic Accreditation of the American Speech-Language-Hearing Association (http://www. asha.org)

In the self-study that universities must complete to gain or keep that accreditation, the section on the clinical practicum is separate from the section on the academic curriculum. The first item of the clinical practicum section questions the appropriateness of the timing of clinical experience and the academic offering, and whether students understand the classroom theory before they must apply it in the clinic. The most striking question asked was, "What learning experiences are provided that actually relate theory and practice?" The other 15 items in the section asked about the mechanics of the link between theory and practice and aspects of the program operation that lead to student learning, such as the adequacy of the clinical sites, supervisory practices, and provision of student feedback. What the section did not do was discuss the nature of the learning that happens on the clinical practicum; the accreditors left that to the department. Another section, however, has questions for the employers at the practicum sites, about the knowledge competencies that students gain in the program. That kind of experiential component is a typical requirement for many high-end professions, from medicine to architecture to law.

As mentioned earlier, some institutions give academic credit for highly structured internships or cooperative education programs. Johnson & Wales University, which has a few U.S. campuses, provides about 2,400 structured internships a year out of its 11,000-student campus in Providence, Rhode Island. Interns have a faculty adviser and receive academic credit from the work with that adviser. In a remarkable commitment, in 2012 Johnson & Wales began to give stipends to support many of students whose internships are unpaid,[8] so they may receive money as well as academic credit. But notice that even they used the academic course structure to award academic credit.

It seems to me that it is time for more work on the development of a well-tuned system for assessing and accrediting learning from experience outside the academic course option. We higher-education institutions

---

8 http://pbn.com/JWU-gets-to-work-on-internships-with-new-4M-fund,70700?print=1

need to be able to say what students learn when they do these activities and not rely solely on their good self-generated e-portfolios, resumes, or recommendation letters they solicit from work supervisors. Some work has been done in this area, as Cavanaugh challenged us to do a few years go, but not nearly enough.

The Digital Badge

Modern digital badges are, in some ways, a throwback to the guild-based certification of knowledge that began with apprenticeships but with a modern twist that they are online. A digital badge provides certification in a narrowly defined area of knowledge, which can be of any type, even small practical skills, such as being able to do specific functions on a spreadsheet. Digital badges are similar to the real-world merit badges I earned in the Boy Scouts. The small cloth patches were proof that I knew the rudiments of first aid, compass-based navigation, or citizenship, to name a few. The work done to earn these badges was checked by adult leaders, and also laid down stepping stones for advancing through the ranks to Eagle Scout. And it was motivating for me to receive them as small rewards (though I never quite made it to the Eagle level). The motivational appeal of badges earned for mastering chunks of knowledge or skill has not been lost on the video-game industry, which includes similar devices in many games as one progresses up through the levels of the game.

Experts have discussed for many years how to design digital badges to certify learning, but the Mozilla Foundation, working with others in 2011, really started promoting them as a form of online certification. Many organizations and companies, including the prestigious John D. and Catherine T. MacArthur Foundation, joined the effort to host the Badges for Lifelong Learning Competition under an umbrella group called the Humanities, Arts, Science, Technology Alliance and Collaboratory (HASTAC, pronounced "haystack"). That contest was succeeded by

HASTAC's annual Digital Media and Learning Competition, which continues to this day.

A 2014 report by the Alliance for Excellent Education highlights how the growing use of digital badge systems supports professional learning for educators and strengthens college and career readiness among young people.[9] The report recommends policies for introducing digital badge programs and safeguards at the state level to ensure that competency-based learning does not cause at-risk students to fall behind their peers, widening achievement gaps.

For our purposes here, the trick going forward will be to apply digital badges to the kinds of learning that experiential education represents. I think that task is best led by the higher education system, not by outside groups, although, clearly, other sectors will not wait if we do not move rapidly. Perhaps the best arrangement is for digital badges to be designed in deep consultation, or better yet in direct partnership, with the industries that will hire our students or the professions that they will enter. I would expect that early digital badges for experiential education would be a supplement to the college transcript and not supplant the sacred text, as Cavanaugh called it. Universities would record the badges alongside students' cooperative education experiences, electronic portfolios, and even online courses completed outside the college or university.

Putting those kinds of experiences into a student's college record should not be any big deal. It is similar to LinkedIn and other social media networks that list resumes that are chock-full of accomplishments outside of college. The question remains, however, whether colleges will someday award academic credit or other institutional certification that will provide an enhanced validity for digital badges. Will the colleges and universities, who are the arbiters of what is learned, thanks to the sacred text of the credit hour, transcript, and accreditation, let the doors of our monastery

---

9 http://all4ed.org/wp-content/uploads/2013/09/DigitalBadges.pdf

swing open? What kinds of outside forces from start-up companies will force those doors open by providing certification of experiences. Without naming companies, I already see evidence of that happening.

Communities of Practice

Leaving the topic of accreditation and the credit hour, another important principle behind experiential education is the presence of the community in almost all forms of such learning. Social learning experts Etienne and Beverly Wenger-Trayner pioneered the term "community of practice," an idea, as they point out, as old as humanity's thinking about itself. On their website,[10] they define communities of practice, simply, as "groups of people who share a concern or a passion for something they do and learn how to do it better as they interact regularly." In a more elaborate definition, Etienne Wenger-Trayner lays out several principles. First, members of the community of practice are committed to its domain. Think of the people in an accounting office that welcome a student as an intern. Not only has the group been together for some time, but they also share a commitment to the field of accounting and to one another to accomplish certain work. Each of us likely belongs to many such groups, switching effortlessly among them, such as when a member of the accounting office leaves for her ski club's weekend in the mountains.

As we discussed in Chapters 12 and 13, the social dynamics of the community of practice, like any group, probably stem from human evolutionary history. We often are not consciously aware of the profound impact of shared experience, nonverbal communication, reflection, and social pressure in our groups. Certainly, those kinds of social dynamics are commonplace in the first community of practice to which our students have adapted, the K-12 educational system, which overlaps with college a great deal, including the class structure of the learning experience.

---

10 http://wenger-trayner.com

Finally, Etienne Wenger-Trayner talks about the practice aspect of the phrase; practice generally includes shared terminology, the work output, the hierarchy, and common facts and theories that are discussed at almost every meeting. That is why a parent or professor, unless he is an accountant, may not want to accompany that student intern in the accounting office to lunch with her team. The companion will neither be part of the community nor share the practice and will likely be bored, despite being proud of the student.

Of course, such disconnects happen all the time. I cannot tell you how many times my wife patiently sat through dinners with my neuroscientist colleagues, as we spun off jargon-filled conversations about neuroanatomy or neuron-related biochemical pathways. In 1985, I published a book with my father entitled *The Neurobiology of Motivation and Reward.* My mother later told me the project practically ruined two family summer vacations at the New Jersey beach house, as dad and I would literally sneak off from the rest of the family to discuss the latest draft, because to do so in front of them was to beg for their tolerance, at best. Communities of practice are everywhere.

Leaving them can also require adjustment. University coordinators for internships or cooperative education are aware that by placing a student into a full-time work setting, they are launching him or her into a much different world than the classrooms that have been familiar since childhood. A student who returns to the classroom after a full-time internship of three or six months must make an adjustment. As mentioned in Chapter 7, I have often had returning students complain about how immature the other students seem, or at least the ones who have yet to experience a stretch of work away from the classroom. Even more surprising, these students sometimes complain about the basic format of classes and exams that now are such a stark contrast to the community of practice they just left. Fortunately, humans are pretty good at adapting to our communities, so those adjustment periods are usually brief.

Why is the community of practice so powerful in experiential education? The answer is probably found in unconscious decision-making and social motivation. As we have discussed several times, the basic purpose for having a discussion group of peers to reflect on an internship or other learning experience is to use the social community to tap into the unconscious brain processes that complement a conscious task such as keeping a journal that is reviewed by a professor. In the group discussion, students relate to one another both verbally and non-verbally. They naturally ponder and evaluate as a group. They motivate each other to think.

Recall David Eagleman's point that we make most of our decisions using our unconscious brain. Also recall as Joshua Greene in *Moral Tribes* and Jonathan Haidt in *The Righteous Mind* pointed out, we think and even make moral decisions in two different modes: unconscious and conscious. If group reflection with the student's peer-based community of practice can provide leverage to deepen his or her reflection, why wouldn't higher education want that? For a student to move back and forth between communities of practice at the workplace and campus may be one of the most intensive learning opportunities of a college career.

There is yet another way to look at the communities of practice in industry and academics: the institutional level. Academic institutions seem to survive longer than for-profit companies. Few businesses anywhere are as old as Harvard University, the oldest university in the United States; yet there are universities overseas that are even older. With longevity, however, may come slow reflexes in adapting to changes in the workplace. That's why, by working with industry, the higher-education community can reap a huge benefit: a better and more timely awareness of how knowledge is being used in the workplace. The last thing we want our colleges to do is to train students to think using yesterday's workplace ideas. Yet the typical isolation of an academic community of practice can lead to just that. Universities often are indeed a disconnected ivory tower. Industry can help create connections by hiring students on paid internships and by setting up exchanges of their personnel with college faculty. Faculty can be encouraged to increase their research collaboration with industry, and industry personnel could do more research, as well as teaching, in the university. Both sides can find ways to work together on projects of mutual interest, especially involving the students who pass between us.

How can the workplace benefit from higher education? Industry needs us, of course, to supply the next generation of educated citizens. University faculties also have immense intellectual talent and creativity that can be valuable resources. Those facts are well known, but my point is that by exchanging students between industry and higher education, we could better educate our citizens while leading to improvements in both sectors' operations. For example, as mentioned a 2014 Gallup-Purdue poll,[11] supported by the Lumina Foundation, of what leads to an engaged worker shows that many of the experiences in college, such as having a mentor or working on a project for more than a semester, are really taken from what we have discussed here as experiential education.

Knowledge Fluency and Workplace Professionalism

Another principle to consider is that, by applying knowledge from the classroom to the workplace, the student gains fluency with that item of knowledge. We all know that students, by applying knowledge, learn how it can be used. If that takes place in a workplace, where it really matters, students tend to give it their full attention.

What intrigues me is that a student, by manipulating that knowledge in a practical way, gains a better understanding of it in the academic sense and can integrate it better into larger intellectual structures. Let's go back to my secondary school days as a Boy Scout and consider the Pythagorean theorem. One day, as I remember, we had to run a rope from the top of a

---

11 https://www.luminafoundation.org/files/resources/galluppurdueindex-report-2014.pdf

twenty-foot flagpole to a stake in the ground fifteen feet away from its base. We had several pieces of rope of different lengths, but rope was precious, and we did not want to cut it unnecessarily. As we debated which rope to try first, someone remembered the Pythagorean theorem. We used it to determine which rope would do the job the first time, with the minimum cut from it. I was impressed: Until that moment the formula for the Pythagorean theorem of $a^2 + b^2 = c^2$ was just a math problem to me. Now I saw how it could really help with my real-world problems. The question is, did I learn something that I could use back in math class? I think I did.

Knowing the right formula, fact, or theory is the kind of thing that makes a person powerful in a work situation. Such a person garners respect; first, for having relevant knowledge, and the more one knows, the better, in today's knowledge economy. I have seen many co-op students at Northeastern go back to their books after a few days on the job.

Second, and most importantly, is the fluency with which the person can use that knowledge. If the person is not fluent, then the question becomes how fast can he or she become so? Anyone who has taught at cooperative education schools will have noticed that when many students return from fulltime work in their field, they seem older, more mature, more powerful. Often they make the best, most passionate students in their subsequent classes. I saw that in my neuroscience classes.

Researchers have also been looking at how experiential education affects students' knowledge. This field of research is still young, so take these ideas as preliminary. It is well known that learning a new task requires all of a person's conscious attention. As mentioned earlier, you cannot have a good conversation with the person teaching you to ride a bicycle for the first time, unless the conversation is about the actual riding itself. The learner's mind is just too occupied with executing the motor skills to keep from falling. After a while, however, the riding skills are so automatic, so fluent, that the rider can focus less on the bicycle and more on the conversation or the scenery.

This lesson about fluency applies to knowledge gained through experiential education.

Consider how a person achieves fluency in a language in which one was not raised (Blog Footnote 14.2).[12] Some say that a person is fluent when he or she dreams in the new language, but the easiest, most obvious clue is when the person no longer translates back to the native language when going from listening to speaking; both processes seem to be in the new language. Much has been written about how much time it takes to get such fluent knowledge. Whether or not mastery requires the 10,000 hours as prescribed by Malcolm Gladwell, there appears to be no substitute for using knowledge gained in the workplace or real-world activity, where communities of practice can reinforce what is learned until it becomes part of the learner, who becomes fluent in its use.

Learning more about this process is an important area of future research, maybe even combining with neuroscience to explore how knowledge from experience connects to classroom knowledge. Obviously, I think answers may be found in the connections between conscious and unconscious decision-making in the brain.

High-Impact Practices

High-impact practices are not a principle *per se*, but they do point to one. In higher education, high-impact practices refer to a variety of practices that boost students' success in college, especially in their increasing the rates of graduating and doing so on time.[13] The American Association of Colleges and Universities (AACU) offer ten high-impact practices:

---

12 Blog footnote 14.2 *Knowledge fluency*, by Marina Vazura and Jim Stellar, posted on 9/2/13 (http://otherlobe.com/knowledge-fluency/). Marina, who speaks four languages, examines how a learner incorporates a simple skill, such as addition in elementary mathematics, into use so that, as in language fluency, the skill becomes part of the learner without conscious thinking or apparent effort.
13 For a more extensive definition, consult the American Association of Colleges and Universities Web site (http://www.aacu.org/leap/hip.cfm) on LEAP, or Liberal Education and America's Promise, and features the work of George Kuh and others via links to relevant reports.

1. First-year seminars and experiences

2. Common intellectual experiences

3. Learning communities

4. Writing-intensive courses

5. Collaborative assignments and projects

6. Undergraduate research

7. Diversity/global learning

8. Service-learning, community-based learning

9. Internships

10. Capstone courses and projects

Before discussing what these high-impact practices have in common, let us consider two stories about high impact practices on students at the classroom level.

The first is from when I was a dean at Northeastern University. My office sponsored a special scholarship that set up several positive circumstances for the approximately four to six students who received it each year (Blog Footnote 14.3).[14] The scholarships not only were an honor, they also gave the students a special independent opportunity to design and execute a project. It provided money that was substantial enough to create a high potential for success, and yet each student had to win a faculty mentor's approval for his or her project before the funds were released. The program also required each student to meet yearly with the alumni donor who sponsored them, which ended up giving the student invaluable mentoring. The scholarship recipients became well known to

---

14 Blog footnote 14.3. *View from a special experiential scholarship program*, by Valerie De Jianne and Jim Stellar posted on 3/4/10 (http://otherlobe.com/view-from-a-special-experiential-scholarship-program/). Experiential programs take students out of their comfort zone in the classroom and force them to act on their own. This program did so by awarding a $5,000 fellowship so the student could execute a project under the advice of a faculty member and with involvement of the alumni donor as a mentor.

the dean's office, which also allowed me to enlist them in fundraising or recruiting talented prospective freshman. All of the recipients were placed in situations that were substantial and authentic, involved communities of practice outside the classroom, and generated work that allowed them to think critically about their chosen fields. They were also picked out from the crowd and given personal responsibility for the entire program, including finding their faculty mentors. For a variety of reasons, I considered this program to be a high-impact practice.

High impact can occur right in the classroom, to be sure, but usually it requires something else to happen—and usually that something else is a form of experiential education that touches the student personally. I already told the story of how my professor got me to do an internship that changed my career path from medicine to neuroscience research, but I have not described the professor's approach. It went something like this: "Jim, when I see you in my neuroscience class, you seem excited and energized, but when I hear you talk about your potential premedical career you sound uninspired." Our interaction began with his astute observation in the classroom; then he connected with me as a mentor, in a high-impact way. Of course, I am not alone in this experience and it can occur even in high school (Blog Footnote 14.4).[15]

Looking again at the ten high-impact practices from the AACU, it is easy to see how they involve this kind of real-world processing, both within the academy and especially outside it, as in internships and the like. The common principle is that the practices actively engage the student in ways that the external world demands, but that the traditional classroom so often does not. I believe that these practices are high impact because they

---

15 Blog Footnote 14.4. *Refining a long term passion in the academy*, by Michaela Tralli and Jim Stellar, posted on 11/14/12 (http://otherlobe.com/refining-a-long-term-passion-in-the-academy/). The student describes the discovery of her passion starting with an academic achievement in high school. As she traces it through college, this experience led to a series of explorations of majors that led to the self-discovery of what she wanted to do. In turn, that discovery ultimately gave her confidence to talk with me about became a personal journey. Here the connections between the classroom and the lessons from personal experience entirely within it seem powerful, which we must not forget as we look outside the classroom for experiential activities to complement what happens inside it.

powerfully engage the mammalian brain processes of unconscious decision-making. A student, sometimes for the first time in his or her education, acts as a whole person in a continuous process over a sustained period. The conscious deliberation of the primate brain works together with the rapid, unconscious, and intuitive decision making of the mammalian brain: Head and heart work together.

While that unity can sometimes happen in the traditional classroom, it often happens outside of it, where it is very important to have one's heart in one's job, so to speak. In that real-world environment, college students respond and grow because they are using both their hearts and their heads.

CHAPTER 15:

Higher-Education Practices and Experiential Education

As noted in the previous chapter, it can be hard to separate practice from principle. A discussion of the practical side of incorporating learning from experience into higher education, as intended here, will inevitably veer into principles. But let's give it a shot.

The first point is that a great deal of practical implementation expertise is available for universities to tap. In the slightly more than a century since the University of Cincinnati formally incorporated cooperative education—or full-time, paid internships—into its academic program, that form of experience-based learning has spread around the world, and it has joined with other forms such as service-learning and study abroad into what we now broadly call experiential education. These diverse experiences offer opportunities for colleges and universities to learn from each other. There is nothing better for an institution that is trying to implement something new than to compare best practices with other relevant institutions. After all, we in higher education have done it very well for centuries with the academic curriculum. Consider the influence we have had on each other ranging from the formation of psychology departments out of philosophy departments beginning in the late 1800s to the creation of departments of neuroscience in my lifetime.

A second point is that all forms of experiential education can bring benefits to the university, as well as to the industries and agencies that employ higher-education graduates. On the higher-education side, students become more mature learners in the classroom by applying what they know, and that can help them to better learn and more likely stay at the university. Experiential education is a high-impact practice, and such practices are known to improve undergraduate student success and therefore retention to graduation,[1] by which today's universities are judged.

Industry also has benefits from participating in experiential education. At a general level, industry can help college students become more mature and ready for work. But there are specific benefits to industry such as new workers with some experiential education in college becoming more productive faster and even staying longer in the company due to a better initial match with the company's actual work. Both effects reduce costs. Simply put, it is sometimes said at cooperative education schools that the ultimate interview is an internship — particularly at technical companies now faced with a need to interact more with people in the modern, business, customer-service world.[2]

To use experiential education to help students get that first job after college or get into further educational programs, we in higher education

---

1 http://nsse.indiana.edu/html/high_impact_practices.cfm
2 This point was made by Mr. Tadahito Yamamoto, Chairman of the Board of Fuji Xerox Co., in a plenary presentation at the 2015 WACE conference in Kyoto (http://www.waceinc.org/kyoto2015/speakers.html). It has been made by many industry leaders.

need to pay better attention to the ways we can work with industry. The goal is to co-create the citizens of tomorrow (Blog Footnote 15.1),[3] and that requires a true partnership, where both higher educational and industry win. Creating that win-win situation for the experiential providers as well as the universities and colleges may be the most important practical point I can think of in implementing and sustaining experiential education programs.

Paid Internships and Title VIII

This industry-academic partnership deserves scrutiny as a practical matter, and one way to do that is to take a brief look at internships historically and today. The willingness in U.S. higher education to relate to industry and respond to its needs has its roots in the mid-1800s. The federal Land Grant Act of 1861 led to the establishment of new colleges with a strong focus on agriculture and other practical fields. Until then, colleges, with the exception of military academies, had focused almost exclusively on academic preparation.

The trend toward advanced practical education was supported by the ideas of the renowned educator and pragmatic philosopher John Dewey (1859-1952). Dewey recognized that learning by doing had value comparable to learning in the classroom. Harvard philosopher and psychologist William James (1842-1910) anticipated those ideas even earlier. Of course, you can also go back to Confucius, 2,500 years ago, who famously wrote, "I hear and I forget; I see and I remember; I do and I understand."

A more recent impetus was Title VIII of the Higher Education Act of 1965. It established government grants to develop programs of cooperative education, defined as, "alternating or parallel periods of

---

3 Blog footnote 15.1 *Industry-academic co-creation*, by Thami Msubo and Jim Stellar, posted on 10/18/09 (http://otherlobe. com/industry-academic-co-creation/) Co-creation in industry means making a product together between two industries as opposed to one buying the raw material from the other and making the product themselves. It is a little dehumanizing to consider the student a product, but the point that industry and the academic establishment should collaborate on generating educated citizens does seem important (and a little nicer).

academic study and public or private employment to give students work experiences related to their academic or occupational objectives and an opportunity to earn the funds necessary for continuing and completing their education."[4]

Sound familiar?

As a few gray-haired veterans of college career-development offices today may remember, many universities long ago established cooperative education programs under Title VIII, only to wind them down about thirty years later when Congress discontinued the funding. Some co-op programs survived. For example, the City University of University of New York (CUNY) kept the LaGuardia Community College co-op program going for many years. Another member of the CUNY system, Queens College, where I worked for five years, folded its cooperative education program back into its career-development center shortly after the funding stopped; and while it still offers internships, the program understandably has not sustained the same level of student or industry participation that one sees in a typical cooperative education college or university.

In the last 10 years, more students at U.S. colleges have been interested internships than ever before,[5] particularly paid internships or co-ops.[6] But that apparent progress is tempered by the fact that unpaid internships have grown at the expense of paid internships. Remember that full-time paid internships, as we discussed in Chapter 7, are educationally powerful in large part because they are both authentic and substantial; unpaid internships score lower in both characteristics, even though they can be very useful if properly monitored by the college or university. Of course, those are just two of the many forms of experiential education we have discussed.

---

4 Section N of the act designated grants of up to $500,000 per consortia of institutions or up to $75,000 per individual institution. http://legcounsel.house.gov/Comps/HEA65_CMD.pdf), pp. 812-17.

5 For a history of internships in U.S. colleges, visit the Cooperative Education and Internship Association website (www.ceiainc.org/history)

6 https://www.naceweb.org/uploadedFiles/Content/static-assets/downloads/executive-summary/2015-internship-co-op-survey-executive-summary.pdf

In my mind, the renaissance in experiential education is driven in part by universities' need to prove the value of their degrees by ensuring student success after graduation and thereby to justify the cost of higher education (Blog Footnote 15.2)[7] in money and time. Experiential education helps them make that case.

Governments in some countries have also gotten involved, doing what the American government did years ago, by supporting cooperative education and thereby brokering partnerships between industry and universities. I have seen this partnership through consulting work I did for the World Association of Cooperative Education[8] in Thailand and in Namibia, where the driver was a governmental attempt to improve the economy. Many other countries have invested in this idea in one form or another from South Africa to Australia. In Europe, national governments have historically strongly supported higher education, and despite recent changes, have perhaps positioned themselves better to support experiential education than in the United States.[9]

To be clear, I am not advocating that American universities would be better off with government funding on the scale of other countries. That is a topic for another book. America has a high level of private colleges and universities, and business entrepreneurship is an important national characteristic that fits well with experiential education implementation. Indeed it might be better for experiential education to rely on partnerships developed between academic institutions and industry so that the programs are well tailored to the needs of both. Yet it is worth looking at ideas and examples from the rest of the world, as well as from America's own historical experience. Sometimes it is true, as in the words of the old song by Peter Allen and Carole Bayer Sager, that "Everything Old Is New Again."

7 Blog footnote 15.2 *College price vs. value and experiential education*, by Allyson Savin and Jim Stellar, posted on 12/20/2012 (http://otherlobe.com/college-price-vs-value-and-experiential-education/). This post discusses the enormous increase in price of a college degree and the toll in terms of debt. It also discusses how experiential education can help students get more value out of the same cost. What may be most interesting is that the same unconscious decision making brain circuits, into which experiential education taps, may also be involved in the decision to take on debt and maybe even participate in a market bubble.
8 www.waceinc.org
9 Yet some changes in public support are occurring in Europe, such as the 1999 Bologna Accords, that parallel the recent history of America where governments everywhere want to pay a bit less for its university education and ask students and families to pay more.

Current Organizations

First, let's look at the busy hive of experiential-education organizations that and is currently available to any educator who wishes to learn more about them. These organizations hold conferences and meetings on the subject, publish reports and guides, hold training institutes, and seek to build networks of national and regional organizations to promote cooperative education and related activities. In addition to the peer learning between colleges and universities, these organizations provide a structural framework for experiential education to advance in higher education. Of course, this activity is dynamic and, by the time you read these words, new organizations may have appeared that you can find with an internet search.

A good place for me to start, due to my familiarity, is the previously mentioned World Association of Cooperative Education (WACE).[10] Founded in 1983, it merged a few years ago with the older American-focused National Commission for Cooperative Education, which itself was formed out of a 1961 report commissioned report by the Ford Foundation.[11] WACE retained its name and today is the only truly global experiential education organization where educational institutions and industry employers meet to compare ideas and operations about how to best educate students.

As an aside, there are many histories of cooperative education, including in a recent book by Yasushi Tanaka in 2014 on the economics of cooperative education,[12] or in various handbooks[13] or journals.[14] But my purpose here is not to provide a history, just to give a feeling for the origin of the current organizations.

My own significant association with these organizations began at WACE in 2003, when I became co-founder and co-director of what ended

---

10 http://www.waceinc.org
11 *Work-study college. programs; appraisal and report of the study of cooperative education,* (James Warner Wilson and Edward H Lyons, New York: Harper 1961.
12 Yasushi Tanaka, *The Economics of Cooperative Education: A practitioner's guide to the theoretical framework and empirical assessment of cooperative education* (Routledge Studies in the Modern World Economy) Routledge Press, NY, 2015.
13 International Handbook for Cooperative and Work-Integrated Education: International Perspectives of Theory, Research and Practice, 2nd Edition. Editors: Richard K. Coll and Karsten E. Zegwaard (http://www.waceinc.org/handbook.html)
14 for example: http://www.apjce.org

up being the WACE Planning Institute for Experiential Education.[15] By 2015, that institute had worked with more than seventy universities, state systems, and countries through its summer program to help them develop academically integrated strategies of experiential education.

Other important national or regional organizations, including the following:

- The Canadian Association for Cooperative Education (CAFCE)[16] as well as provincial organizations

- The Thailand Association of Cooperative Education (TACE)[17]

- The Australian Collaborative Educational Network (ACEN)[18]

- The Southern Africa Society for Cooperative Education (SASCE)[19]

- New Zealand Association for Cooperative Education (NZACE)[20]

Higher education organizations in Europe and other world regions also include societies that are interested in cooperative education.

To return to WACE, as of this writing, it has satellite offices at the University West in Sweden and at Suranaree University of Technology in Thailand. Both have been active recently. The first WACE conference on research was held at University West in 2014 and a planning institute was held at an independent site in Thailand in late 2015. Interestingly, both universities have new programs that give a PhD degree in the study of cooperative education. A more recent and second research conference was held in June of 2016 in Victoria, British Columbia.

In the United States, a number of organizations exist to promote learning from experience in higher education, some of them with long histories. Some examples include:

15 http://www.waceinc.org/institute
16 http://www.cafce.ca
17 http://www.tace.or.th
18 http://www.acen.edu.au
19 http://www.sasce.net
20 http://www.nzace.ac.nz

- The Cooperative Education Internship Association[21]

- The National Association of Colleges and Employers[22]

- The National Society for Experiential Education[23]

- The Council for Adult and Experiential Learning[24]

Organizations that promote experiential education in specific disciplines are too numerous to list. Some standouts include the Cooperative and Experiential Education Division of the American Society for Engineers,[25] and the Association to Advance Collegiate Schools of Business (AACSB).[26] The AACSB holds seminars on experiential education. I'll also mention my own scholarly discipline, the Society for Neuroscience, which has an affiliated group that supports undergraduate research and other educational activities called the Faculty for Undergraduate Neuroscience.[27] I did not list the organizations around the world that do the same because they are numerous, and I think you get the point.

A simple web search on "experiential education" will turn up even more organizations, more programs, and much more writing on the subject. Do the same with the search terms "internships," "service-learning," or any specific area of experiential education and you will be flooded with resources. You also will notice that many programs are embedded in centers or institutes, some of them associated with teaching centers or with study-abroad offices, career centers, or other specific activities. An interesting example is the President's Promise office at the University of Maryland,[28] an office that helps students engage in experiential education, to integrate different forms with one another and academics, and "to make meaning of these experiences so they can be articulated to employers upon graduation."[29]

---

21 http://www.ceiainc.org
22 http://www.naceweb.org
23 http://www.nsee.org
24 http://www.cael.org
25 http://ceed.asee.org
26 http://www.aacsb.edu
27 http://www.funfaculty.org
28 http://www.careercenter.umd.edu
29 http://www.presidentspromise.umd.edu

Virtually all of the schools that are dedicated to experiential learning have a central office to organize their program. One of the functions of such an office is to help the institution gather information and conduct studies to better understand the best practices or the underlying theory of learning in these disciplines. Their staff and faculty members attend conferences, publish in journals, and disseminate information on their websites.

Building Experiential Education Programs

How does an institution build a program of experiential education? A solid program is not merely a collection of outside experiences that are relevant to a conventional academic curriculum, though such piecemeal activities can still benefit students. No single approach will work for every college; the best method will be different for community service, abroad programs, or industry internships.

It has become the norm for every higher education institution to have a strategic plan. Accreditation agencies want to see that the institution they are examining has a strategic plan. They also ask want to see that the plan is supported by the university budget, is used to make program decisions, and is supported and driven by the collection of relevant data about student learning. Any experiential education effort that is not in the university's strategic plan and tied to student learning will likely remain minor, even if it is important to individual students.

Strategic planning of any type demands buy-in from the faculty, a committed and durable leadership, and the need to allocate resources accordingly. I do not have all the answers about how to achieve those elements, but I have some insights from being a senior academic leader at three higher education institutions, co-directing the Experiential Education Institute for over nine years, consulting with universities and the governments of Thailand and Namibia, and participating actively in WACE. The following are some of my thoughts based on that experience. I grouped them into five areas below and I will keep them very brief, as each could be its own chapter.

1) The Strategic Plan

As mentioned a number of times before, my college mentor advised me to take an internship. He did so not because he was following a university strategic plan but because he thought it would be good for me. It worked, but few were as lucky as me to have such a mentor. A strategic plan that included internships — if it was widely discussed on campus and developed through a standard adoption process — helps harness the power of the college for all of its students. Leadership from the top is important, but as stated above, buy-in from the base of students, faculty, and administrators at the operational level of the university or college is critical. The strategic plan is one way to get that buy-in.

2) Faculty Buy-in

A strategic plan does nothing unless enough of the faculty and key staff buy into it and make it a natural part of the institution. To put that point another way, the people in the institution have to be aligned with a plan that includes experiential education, or its implementation will have insufficient power. To do that, one has to change the way resources are allocated. The largest allocation of any college or university is to faculty salaries and faculty express the institution's purpose through the classical work of teaching courses. One does not need to change that classroom work, but one does need to develop recourses to support faculty, where they are interested, in promoting experiential education.

It is a challenge to combine academics with outside class experiences in the classroom or to make space for it in the curricular or co-curricular activities of a department. Professors bring to bear the prestige of their discipline and the status of tenure to the priorities that the institution sets. On the other hand, professors who have not bought into the plan can try wait it out or even actively undermine it and its supporters. Fortunately, experiential education aims to enhance student learning and success, and most faculty members I have met in my career really do care about enhancing student learning.

3) Alignment - Leadership from All Levels

I have already told the story about how, my Northeastern University colleagues and I read Jim Collins' book, *Good to Great*, as we were trying to figure out how Northeastern could move forward under then-President Richard Freeland. Over the next few years, I saw us applying many of Collins' ideas about skilled leadership. Yet even as I realized the importance of having leadership around a strategic idea, I also read *Connecting the Dots: Aligning Projects with Objectives in Unpredictable Times*, a 2003 book by Cathleen Benko and F. Warren McFarlan.[30] That book showed me how a powerful synergy could result from the alignment between the small things that individual members of the institution do and the larger strategic direction of the institution.

Alignment is hard to achieve, but once it starts to happen, a productive passion can spread through the institution, much like Simon Sinek talks about in the 2009 book, *Start With Why: How Great Leaders Inspire Everyone To Take Action*.[31] I felt that passion at Northeastern, as we were moving to the next level of quality and reputation. While I would like to explore the neuroscience of how building passion fits with unconscious decision-making processes in the mammalian social brain, that is another book, so I will leave this discussion here.

---

30 Harvard Business School Press, Boston, MA, 2003.
31 Penguin Group, New York, NY, 2009

4) Resources

Given leadership, the plan, and alignment, the effort also requires resources. Sometimes a program takes off because a donor makes a transformative gift to construct a building or endow a school or program. In most cases, the university itself makes a concerted effort over a long period of time to generate those resources, perhaps through increased retention or improved recruitment of new students that can sustain the necessary investment. I was once told that if someone wants to understand the university's actual strategic plan versus the one in the fancy brochure, they should look at the university's budget. That study makes clear the contrast between institutional leaders in experiential education and others. Some institutions have had a budgetary commitment over decades, and others are trying now to catch up. The real magic of institutional transformation happens when the effort is sustained and the university begins to reap the payback of successful graduates and a rising reputation.

5) Assessing Student Success

The presumed link between experiential activities and student retention—that is, keeping students in college and preferably at the same college through to graduation—is tantalizing and important. Logically, if an undergraduate can see the value of college to his or her future career, and if that is a positive vision, then that student gains a personal momentum that can help them overcome the obstacles like academic setbacks and life events that might otherwise be discouraging. For this reason too, we have to figure out what is going on in the experiential activities just like we do in our courses in the curriculum. Outside organizations want to help (e.g. WACE runs an assessment institute).[32]

An equally beneficial but different outcome is if the experience helps a student discover that he or she is on the wrong path. That realization

---

32 http://www.waceinc.org/drexel2015/index.html

may avert a costly mistake in graduate school and help students find a field of study and future work that is a better match for their interests and talents. It can be painful to switch directions at the time, but I heard a lot from older alumni, particularly at Northeastern University, that such a career trajectory altering experience was one of the greatest gifts from their undergraduate education.

Building on Student Commitment

How students commit to their majors and hold onto that commitment is a subject that we need to discuss. To just begin that topic, let's first consider the example of higher the *Berufsakademie* model in Germany of technical education that is based on a deep integration of academia and industry where the student makes the commitment. Then let's look at a University of Cincinnati program designed to fine-tune the course content based on employer feedback to meet a committed student's needs. In both cases, the idea is to have good integration between the student's two sets of experiences.

The *Berufsakademie* program started in the 1970s and is one of the world's most robust models of cooperative education. In it students complete a higher education program that alternates between three months of training on the job as an employee in industry with a comparable period of study at a university. Interestingly, they are admitted to both institutions at the start of their college career. Students experience the workplace and the university as equal partners in their training and support—an arrangement that puts the student in charge of the process of acquiring knowledge, as he or she must to apply it to both institutions.

In the classroom, the situation is classically highly refined with a clear description of course content and with fair announced tests to measure learning of the course material. In the workplace, the situation is much more unpredictable, complex, real-world, and engaging. At work, the right answer is more in the outcome of a project in which the student is involved, and how he or she helped the team get a successful result. In the program, these two experiences are tailored to overlap and reinforce each other with rapid frequent alternation between the forms requiring good communication between both entities. Research suggests that the *Berufsakademie* program leads to higher salaries for young employees and more rapid advancement into management positions, compared to other forms of education.[33]

The other example is based on work done and published by Cheryl Cates and Kettil Cedercreutz of the University of Cincinnati.[34] Their 2008 report came out of a multi-year study supported by a U.S. government grant from the Fund for the Improvement of Postsecondary Education that was matched with support from their university. The team used employer feedback from thousands of annual evaluations of students who took part in the standard Cincinnati cooperative education program, where full-time work alternated repeatedly with full-time university study. The students were from four different departments in different colleges of the University of Cincinnati. The employment feedback data was used to inform departments on how their students were doing at the workplace on necessary skills, such as writing.

The researchers' mathematical analysis is beyond the scope of this book, but essentially, the study created a feedback loop to the curricular design of the departments, showing whether certain specific elements of the curricula were working in terms of employer satisfaction with the student's skills. It also showed how the students grew during the educational process, and where changes in the student's dual education from the university and the industry might be made. That sort of data could not only guide the improvement of educational practices, but the better fit of these two experiences can give students confidence that they are in the right institution in the right program, which is half the challenge of retention.

---

33 Article by Axel Göhringer, 2002. http://www.apjce.org/files/APJCE_03_2_53_58.pdf
34 "Leveraging Cooperative Education to Guide Curricular Innovation: The Development of a Corporate Feedback System for Continuous Improvement." http://www.uc.edu/propractice/ceri/publications.html

Graduation Rates

In the popular rankings of colleges, the definition of student success is influenced strongly by the graduation rate, or the percentage of students who enroll as freshmen and then graduate from the same university within a standard time. Graduation rates are typically calculated for the four-year university at four years and also at six years, which permits a two-year allowance for unexpected circumstances. In the 2015, the dominant ranking entity, *U.S. News & World Report,* gave a university's graduation rate a weight of a little more than 20 percent in its final ranking calculation—about the same weight given to the reputation scores by college and university leaders. But it also gave an additional 7.5 percent retention weight to colleges that outperformed the expected graduation rate based on the characteristics of their entering class of students, making retention the largest factor in determining their ranking that year.

One way for a university to graduate more of its undergraduates is to make a good start with new freshman and new transfer students. Given the importance of retention, there has been much research in that area, and some organizations exist to help shape related programs. One organization that does both is the John Gardner Institute for Excellence in Undergraduate Education.[35] When I served as provost at Queens College, I co-led a Gardner Institute program and hoped for a large boost in retention for three reasons: first, to serve our students well; second, to signal publicly that we were an excellent institution; and third, to keep the tuition revenue of retained students that would create new opportunities for our entire academic community.

Retention has become an important national topic, with calls to promote college attendance and success. Major foundations are offering to contribute to finding solutions. It will come as no surprise that I think experiential education programs can enhance retention and, along with other

---

35 http://www.jngi.org

high impact programs such as university-organized learning communities or powerful student organizations to help students get to off to a good start in college (Blog Footnote 15.3).[36]   A good start with a good group may be important, particularly in diverse student populations (Blog Footnote 15.4).[37] I mention diversity here only briefly, but that topic is important and deserves significant attention in the study of how experiential education can promote student success-perhaps in another book.

Entrepreneurship

Higher education has long had an interest in entrepreneurship, even outside of business schools where it tends to thrive. Entrepreneurship has gained new importance in recent years, however, given the changes in the job market. The time is long gone when a college graduate joined a company and stayed for life. Now many students want to start their own company.   Another factor in developing student interest is the evolution of technology related to e-commerce, social media, mobile, and other new forms of communication. Foundations and corporations have encouraged the trend. Clearly, young people are interested. In a 2011 Gallup poll, some 45 percent of grade-school students who would reach college in the next 10 years said they wanted to start their own business.[38] On campus, you can feel it. Entrepreneurship programs are rising. Students are taking them, but they also are doing it on their own. In 2015, my current institution, the University at Albany, SUNY, won a major grant from the Blackstone Foundation[39] to create entrepreneurship experiences for all students on campus.

---

36 Blog Footnote 15.3. *A Student Group Can Produce Retention – an Example of the Middle Earth Program*, by Marc Cohen and Jim Stellar, posted on 2/2/16 (http://otherlobe.com/a-student-group-can-produce-retention-an-example-of-the-middle-earth-program/). Middle Earth is a peer program at the University at Albany SUNY, which claims a very high freshman-to-sophomore retention rate. Based on interviews with program participants, this post examines why and how it works.
37 Blog Footnote 15.4. *Lessons learned for retention from the EOP program and other student voices*, by Chrisel Martinez, Brittanyliz Echevarria, and Jim Stellar, posted on 11/11/15 (http://otherlobe.com/lessons-learned-for-retention-from-the-eop-program-and-other-student-voices/). The EOP (Educational Opportunity Program) serves a financially challenged, largely minority population where one might expect retention and graduation rates to be lower than the average at University at Albany SUNY. Instead the freshman-to-sophomore retention rates are much higher in EOP, perhaps due to the family-like group dynamics established by the program. The post also examines similar potential needs in the general student population from focus groups that could elevate general student success and the retention/graduation rates that go with it.
38 http://www.gallup.com/poll/150077/students-entrepreneurial-energy-waiting-tapped.aspx
39 https://blackstonelaunchpad.org and http://www.albany.edu/news/66615.php

Students who have internships in business naturally gain practical entrepreneurship experience that enriches any academic study they do in the subject. But entrepreneurship is open to students from a much wider field than one might expect. A local high-tech recruiter who visited my campus recently to recruit students said that he was looking specifically for graphic design majors and music majors for small computer-tech companies. The recruiter told me that, rather than young people with a certain skill set, he was seeking an attitude-the confidence that came from trying things in the real world. He wanted to bring some of that attitude to his client companies.

"Attitude" is a keyword, marking the overlap between entrepreneurship and experiential education. At least that is the case in a college environment, where the students are in a high-growth stage of their lives. This is where the mammalian brain of unconscious decision-making again enters my thinking. Learning is not so much about the fact and theories one has stored from all the classes one has taken. It is about applying that information to something new, even oneself.

Summary

A student who does a freshman-year service project and who discovers something about himself or herself is well on the way to enhanced personal growth. We know that from the Gallup-Purdue poll[40] that examined the results of many experiential-education activities. Such programs can channel the growth of college students and add to the their confidence. As other students complete similar projects and experiences, their departments and even the entire campus will be elevated by their new maturity and purpose. And as enough students go through and integrate learning from experiential and entrepreneurship programs, they may turn back to the business of running the campus itself, even as students, improving innovation in higher education, and maybe making it more experiential. That sounds to me like a virtuous cycle.

---

40 http://products.gallup.com/168857/gallup-purdue-index-inaugural-national-report.aspx

Afterword

I want you to remember three things from this book.

First, your mind is driven by your brain, and the human brain is the most awesome organizational structure that the world has ever seen. That little organ in your head not only can do so much, but it can change its own structure and function. To me, that capacity for change is a fundamentally optimistic message for higher education. You are not limited by who you are. You can develop new skills as well as learn new knowledge. You can be transformed. It just takes a lot of work.

The second thing I want you to remember is that passion is key to transformative learning. It is important to doing anything that is a challenge, and to get passion requires that we in higher education go beyond our students' conscious learning to engage what have called their mammalian brain. The mammalian brain responds to emotion, people, and loves the real world. It strongly influences important decisions we make such as which major best suits the college student, and it does so largely outside of conscious thinking.

The problem with higher education is that over centuries of refinement, we just about sucked the real-world life out of it, at least for the average student. Don't get me wrong. The ivory tower is where I spent my entire professional life, and it is beautiful. Higher education has produced very real advances in the world and it is worth the substantial investment of time and resources that society has made. But adding experiential education can make it even better, and we discussed in this book the many ways in which higher education can do that.

Third, learning from experience is a very old form of learning whose time has come again. In an era where so many people question the price and the value of higher education, why would we not welcome this help? I can tell you from my direct observation that this form of education takes nothing away from the highest goals of academic learning. I have seen the combination of academic and experiential education galvanize my students and put them into the best medical and graduate schools in America. I have seen it transform a college and a university. It is more complex than a classical college program of study, but it is worth it.

I like saying that in higher education, and will say again, we need to row the boat with both oars. Content knowledge is one oar and we are good at that. The other oar is passion, commitment, and a real-world sense of how that content knowledge works for the individual student while they are in college. That kind of knowledge comes from them applying the content they are learning to their developing lives.

Higher education is up to the challenge. We can engage with the world outside of the ivory tower without losing our integrity and our power. If we do that, we will grow as an industry. Our students will be better. And then we can all row the boat with both oars.

Index